BECAUSE BORING IS GOOD

# ORDINARY STEPS

for Creating an Extraordinarily Boring, Niche Business

## SCOTT J. FORMAN

# ORDINARY STEPS

## for Creating an Extraordinarily Boring, Niche Business

Ordinary Steps for Creating an Extraordinarily Boring, Niche Business

Copyright © 2023 by Scott J. Forman

All rights reserved. No part of this publication may be reproduced, distributed, or transmitted in any form or by any means, including photocopying, recording, or other electronic or mechanical methods, without the prior written permission of the author, except in the case of brief quotations embodied in critical reviews and certain other noncommercial uses permitted by copyright law.

Disclaimer:
The author strives to be as accurate and complete as possible in the creation of this book, notwithstanding the fact that the author does not warrant or represent at any time that the contents within are accurate due to the rapidly changing nature of the Internet.

While all attempts have been made to verify information provided in this publication, the Author and the Publisher assume no responsibility and are not liable for errors, omissions, or contrary interpretation of the subject matter herein. The Author and Publisher hereby disclaim any liability, loss or damage incurred as a result of the application and utilization, whether directly or indirectly, of any information, suggestion, advice, or procedure in this book. Any perceived slights of specific persons, peoples, or organizations are unintentional.

In practical advice books, like anything else in life, there are no guarantees of income made. Readers are cautioned to rely on their own judgment about their individual circumstances to act accordingly. Readers are responsible for their own actions, choices, and results. This book is not intended for use as a source of legal, business, accounting or financial advice. All readers are advised to seek the services of competent professionals in legal, business, accounting, and finance field.

Printed in the United States of America

Book Cover and Interior Formatting by 100 Covers

ISBN: 979-8-9885927-0-9

# CONTENTS

**2021: The Signing** ........................................ xi
    Odds of Success for a StartUp. ................... xiii
    Proven, but, Boring Process ....................... xiv

**Chapter 1: Be An *Investigative* News Reporter** ....... 1
    Seeing the World Differently ....................... 4
    What Sparks You? .................................... 5
    How Boring Is Your Business? ...................... 7
    Exciting Business Ideas ............................. 8
        Extraordinary Business Table ................. 9
    First W: Who ....................................... 14
    Second W: What ..................................... 15
    Third W: When ...................................... 16
    Fourth W: Where .................................... 17
    Fifth W: Why ....................................... 19
    One H: How - well, not quite yet.................. 21
    Chapter 1 Checklist................................. 22

## Chapter 2: Identify a Business that Suits You & Answers Your 1 H - How .............................. 23
- Childhood. ............................................................. 23
  - Key questions to answer. ................................. 25
    - Partnerships............................................... 27
- Money, Money, Money. ....................................... 28
- Funding Options ................................................. 30
  - 1) Self, friends, or family funding ................... 30
  - 2) Business loan/selling business ownership..... 32
    - The Founder's Approaches. ....................... 34
  - 3. Royalty/License/Creative Deal .................. 36
- What is Success? What is Failure? What's for Dinner? .... 39
- Chapter 2 Checklist. ............................................ 42

## Chapter 3: Within the Boring Niches, Lie the Real Riches ...... 43
- How To Find a Boring Niche? ............................. 44
  - Market Research: TAM, SAM, SOM, and the Band Played On. ................................ 45
    - Total Addressable Market (TAM) .............. 45
    - Serviceable Available Market (SAM). ........ 46
    - Serviceable Obtainable Market (SOM) ...... 72
  - Example - My Imaginary Pie Business. ......... 46
  - What was our niche? .................................... 59
  - Enlist Help - Read, Listen, Watch, Socialize ..... 60

Help Yourself First.................................................. 62
    Websites that Offer Free Courses...................... 63
    Creative Sources for Help ................................. 63
Chapter 3 Checklist................................................. 65

## Chapter 4: Complete Your Business Plan .................. 67
Business Plan Sections........................................... 68
    Executive Summary........................................... 68
    Company Description........................................ 69
    Market Analysis................................................ 70
        Why Not Your Competition? ......................... 72
        Hierarchy of Business Differentiators............ 74
    Organization and Management........................ 77
    Service or Product Line ................................... 79
    Marketing and Sales......................................... 79
    Funding request................................................ 81
    Financial projections ....................................... 82
    Appendix ........................................................... 84
Chapter 4 Checklist................................................. 85

## Chapter 5: How to Build Your Product or Service ...... 87
Input ===> Throughput ===> Output........................ 88
    Inputs................................................................ 88
    Throughput....................................................... 90

  Output . . . . . . . . . . . . . . . . . . . . . . . . . . . . . . . . . . . 91
 Project Schedule/Checklist . . . . . . . . . . . . . . . . . . . . . . 93
  Sample Project Schedule - Build Prototype. . . . . . . . . . 95
  Sample Schedule for Consultative Service Business . . . . 98
 Starting a company - Basic Needs. . . . . . . . . . . . . . . . . 100
 Chapter 5 Checklist. . . . . . . . . . . . . . . . . . . . . . . . . . . 106

## Chapter 6: Sales & Marketing: Who Are You?.. . . . . . . 107
 Marketing Plan . . . . . . . . . . . . . . . . . . . . . . . . . . . . . 108
  Target Market . . . . . . . . . . . . . . . . . . . . . . . . . . . . . 109
  Competitive Advantage .. . . . . . . . . . . . . . . . . . . . . . 109
  Sales Plan .. . . . . . . . . . . . . . . . . . . . . . . . . . . . . . . 109
   How do you sell to your customers? . . . . . . . . . . . 110
   Sales Strategies. . . . . . . . . . . . . . . . . . . . . . . . . . 110
  Marketing and Sales Goals . . . . . . . . . . . . . . . . . . . 112
   What Does Brand Awareness Include? . . . . . . . . . . 113
   Sales/Marketing Material Highlighting
   Your Business .. . . . . . . . . . . . . . . . . . . . . . . . . . 113
   Phone and email templates. . . . . . . . . . . . . . . . . . 114
  Marketing Action Plan .. . . . . . . . . . . . . . . . . . . . . . 114
  Budget. . . . . . . . . . . . . . . . . . . . . . . . . . . . . . . . . . 115
  Measure and Update the Plan.. . . . . . . . . . . . . . . . . 116
  Don't Forget About Operations.. . . . . . . . . . . . . . . . 116
 Chapter 6 Checklist. . . . . . . . . . . . . . . . . . . . . . . . . . 118

## Chapter 7: Customer On-Boarding ... 119

Customer On-Boarding: Relationship Building
By A Different Name ... 120

Optimized Customer Experience ... 121

Example: Mike's Journey As a New Customer ... 122

Prospective Customer Journey ... 125

Changes to Dennis's Gym Processes ... 126

Prospective Customers Gym Journey ... 128

Successful Relationship Building Between
Company and Customer ... 131

Prospect and Customer Profile ... 133

Complete Customer Journey For Dennis's Gym ... 134

Chapter 7 Checklist ... 136


## Chapter 8: Customer Retention-A Bird In the Hand ... 137

Determine Customer Sentiment ... 139

1) Internal Customer Review ... 139

2) Request Customer Feedback ... 141

Discussion and Survey Questions ... 142

Ongoing Maintenance ... 143

Who Interacts with the Customer? ... 143

How Balanced Is Your Team? ... 145

How Do You Interact with Customers? ... 146

Chapter 8 Checklist ... 154

## Chapter 9: Business Optimization: Future Resistant .......... 155

How to Become Future Resistant........................ 156

Business Optimization ............................ 157

1) Market Research ............................ 157

2) Demographic Analysis ....................... 161

3) Imaginary Pivots ........................... 170

4) Reduce or Remove Debt...................... 173

5) Offer Unique Incentives ..................... 175

Profit-based Bonus Pool ..................... 175

Collaboration ............................... 177

Chapter 9 Checklist.............................. 178

## Chapter 10: Keep Growing Your Biz or Sell? ............ 181

Who Are You Without Your Business? ............... 182

Continue to Grow Your Business..................... 183

Sell the Business.................................. 185

Queen for a Day.............................. 186

Chapter 10 Checklist.............................. 189

# 2021
# THE SIGNING

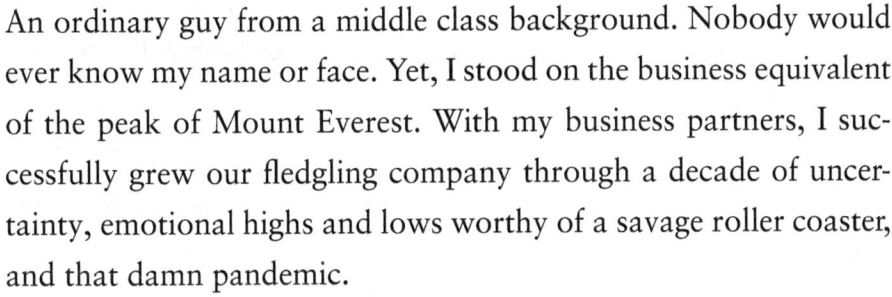

An ordinary guy from a middle class background. Nobody would ever know my name or face. Yet, I stood on the business equivalent of the peak of Mount Everest. With my business partners, I successfully grew our fledgling company through a decade of uncertainty, emotional highs and lows worthy of a savage roller coaster, and that damn pandemic.

Due diligence was finished, and the closing documents delivered. We were the biggest underdog in our industry, and yet we took on the great giants and won. One of them decided competing against us wasn't worth it any longer, so they bought us instead. I was raised to be humble and not brag, but please give me this moment. This was an extraordinary out-of-body experience. After all, I was the same person who in elementary school dealt with several teachers who gave up on me as someone not worth the effort to teach. Fortunately, my parents believed in me, until I believed in me, and through hard work, determination, and perseverance, I made it. The company I gave a good portion of my life and time to, made it.

When starting the company, I was told by many that we wouldn't make it as the odds were too stacked against us. They weren't wrong about the odds. Once we were acquired, some of those same people said how strong our company was and how they always knew we had something. There aren't many compliments in the business world, just results. These were compliments, and we took them.

As I digitally signed the agreement that culminated my life's work, I shook my head thinking that this process was far different than I had expected. I expected trumpets or a mariachi band, a crowd full of supporters cheering me on, as I crossed the finish line winning an impossible race. I expected the chanting from the 1980 USA hockey victory over the Soviet Union "USA, USA". Instead I got the hospital sterility of a clean room. Just me and my thoughts clicking through a digital contract. I wasn't fully alone though; holding the dog tag containing my dad's ashes just months after he passed, I continued to click through the agreement.

"We did it, Dad," I said as I submitted the document.

THE SIGNING

# ODDS OF SUCCESS FOR A STARTUP

How does an ordinary person start a business? Don't they know that the chances of failure far exceeds that of success? The latest available private company survivorship numbers from the Bureau of Labor Statistics (BLS)[1] provide the same averages you're likely to find whether you go back or forward 50 years. It's like the law of large numbers[2], the more times you flip the coin, the more likely you are to hit a 50/50 probability of getting heads or tails.

As shown in the referenced BLS statistics, the business equivalent for this law is no different. 10-20% of businesses fail within the first two years. Nearly half of businesses fail within the first five years and about two-thirds close down within ten years. More difficult to calculate are the chances of building a multi-million dollar business that generates enough net income to support the families of employed founders, and the families of their employees. Using the referenced data provided by BLS, as well as other data sources[3] from the Census Bureau, it is likely that the odds of successfully building a multi-million dollar business in net income, from scratch, is pretty low; building a business like this, which also survives for at least 5-10 years, must have odds in the single digits. Then, if you go even further and determine what percentage of those businesses continue to scale to grow into massively larger companies? My best guess is that you're now looking at odds that are equivalent to winning the lottery or getting struck by lightning. In fact, according to this article[4], the odds are 0.00006% of growing your company to a billion dollar company.

So why start a business, you wonder? The odds are horribly against you and it seems like it's just dumb luck if you succeed when all is said and done.

I guess the answer is that we do it for the same reason we do anything in life that's risky, we want a chance to improve our life. As for luck, yes, that is obviously a part of the equation. But equally critical to luck are hard work, perseverance, dedication, and flexibility.

When it comes to building a successful business, you may inquire, is the process repeatable? Can anyone do it? The answers are yes and yes. But if you want to increase your chances of success instead of relying on luck, you need help. Help which comes in the form of a proven process that is repeatable.

## PROVEN BUT BORING PROCESS

This book provides a proven process that I have used successfully throughout my career of over 30 years in building and managing multiple products and programs. I have been involved with several start-ups throughout my career both as an employee and a consultant. Most importantly I used the process contained in this book in starting my own company, with partners, to build up and successfully sell our business.

The process contained in this book works well for one simple reason, it is boring and time consuming. There is no short-cut, just roll up your sleeves and do the work. Although the process cannot guarantee success, it can guarantee that you will increase your probability of success.

My description of the process reminds me of an answer Warren Buffet provided to Jeff Bezos in a meeting when asked why everyone doesn't copy his simple investing style. Buffet said, "Because nobody wants to get rich slow[5]." In other words, his style was too boring for others.

Buffett knows boring works, and it works especially well for creating a special or extraordinary business. Why? Because, as Buffet intimated, nobody wants to be part of a boring business just as nobody wants to get rich slowly. Most people want social media stardom replete with daily "my life in a day" video vignettes, power lunches, and huge business meetings with stars.

I don't know how to do any of that. However, I do know how to build a boring, niche business that will take years for you to build up, support yourself and others, and provide you with the kind of independence that can only come from your business's success.

Like me, nobody may know your name or what you did because your business is boring. But you don't care about that. You will own your time and breathe easier when you climb atop the peak of Business Mount Everest because you did it! And if you want to, you can do it again.

## ORDINARY STEPS FOR CREATING AN EXTRAORDINARILY BORING, NICHE BUSINESS

At the beginning of building our company, I turned to one of my partners and said, "There are risks, and there are risks worth taking and this is a risk worth taking." His reply was, "The only risk is not doing this as eventually everyone gets fired." Of course, he was right. Much like any experienced business person will tell you, in business you are only as good as your last close, project, meeting, etc. Put another way, everyone eventually gets fired so you might as well start your own business and make your independence happen. If your business fails, the worst that happens is you end up firing yourself. Hopefully you do so with more grace and support than corporate America.

Welcome to the first day of building your extraordinarily boring, niche business!

# CHAPTER 1
# BE AN INVESTIGATIVE NEWS REPORTER

Depending on when you were born, images brought to your mind when you hear the term "news reporter" will differ. The term may convey an attractive person in front of a video camera, microphone in-hand explaining a dire situation. It may also bring to mind a frumpy person with a notepad shouting questions while scribbling on the notepad.

Regardless of the image, the term connotes a person who is searching for answers. Answers arise when asking the right questions. The right questions begin with the five Ws and one H. The five Ws are "who, what, when, where, why" and the one H is "how."

Answer six simple questions to begin your journey on building your boring business.

But first, we need to shift our mindset a bit more by adding one more word. The word is investigative. Think like an investigative news reporter and ideas will take quick form. Close your eyes for a moment and think back to the most boring task you did yesterday. Retrace your steps.

Maybe you went to the gym or your pantry for a snack, or met a friend somewhere. Now, retrace your steps, moment-by-moment. Think carefully, were there any parts of your journey that could have been improved along the way? Let's say that the most boring thing you did yesterday was to meet a friend for lunch. In this example, your retraced steps might look something like the following:

1) Got dressed.
2) Contacted my friend to agree on meeting time and place.
3) Started the car.
4) Drove to lunch.
5) Found a parking spot.
6) Walked into the restaurant.
7) Met my friend.
8) Ate, drank, and talked.
9) Paid for the meal.
10) Drove home.

In this one tiny example, we have multiple boring business ideas that were constructed from the above normal routine. Here they are:

1) Restaurant picking apps that allow you to easily pick restaurants jointly, either randomly or with specific filters.

2) Scheduling apps that enable multiple people to collaboratively pick a meeting place and time.

3) Clothing apps that help select and ship new outfits on an ongoing basis.

4) Clothing selection apps that display and suggest the perfect outfit for any occasion.

5) Parking spot reservation apps where you can reserve a parking spot ahead of time for a small fee or pay in advance for the spot, where applicable.

6) Restaurant reservation apps to mitigate waiting times.

7) Apps to suggest the best meals, drinks, or time to go to the restaurant where you're meeting your friend.

8) Navigational apps that provide the best route to travel to meet your friend. Your personalized driving route is based on multiple factors, including the time of the meeting and your road preferences.

9) Nutrition apps that enable you to track your food or plan ahead of time what you are going to eat to assist you with portion control or overall health concerns.

10) Payment splitting apps, tip determination apps, and restaurant payment apps that enable you to pay and earn loyalty points.

Note that these are only some of the ideas that we derive from this simple exercise. The point is that in our daily lives there are endless opportunities to help ourselves and others in multiple ways. The more beneficial the help we provide to ourselves and others, the greater the probability that there is a business waiting to be created.

Each of the above business ideas are what I would call boring but they may also be called mundane, ordinary, trite, or dull. The point is that none of these business ideas are glamorous, yet they all belong to extraordinary businesses. Several of these businesses have grown from a simple idea to leading companies or new industries on their own. The Total Addressable Market (TAM) for scheduling apps is well over $500 million, health and nutrition apps that help with portion control and tracking are over one billion dollars, while restaurant reservation services are over two billion dollars. Each of the above businesses make money within rapidly growing industries that didn't exist a short number of years ago.

## SEEING THE WORLD DIFFERENTLY

Being an investigative news reporter allows you to see the world differently. From the moment you awake to the moment you fall asleep, the 5 Ws and 1 H questions for businesses are all around you waiting for interaction.

How do you start? You start. Simple as that. With your investigative news reporter hat on, the world becomes yours to investigate. What things do you or others do daily that interest you? Every product, program or business idea that I've worked on was based on fulfilling needs. Needs that make a customer's life easier or better somehow. You start by identifying common needs which save time, money or solve problems. With nearly eight billion people in our world, each who thinks they are unique but have the same set of common needs waiting to be fulfilled, the odds can heavily be in your favor.

## WHAT SPARKS YOU?

An investigative news reporter sees everything through the lens of the 5 Ws and 1 H and so must you as you begin this journey. Once you identify something that interests, or sparks you, start answering the 5 Ws and 1 H.

Let's say that you are interested in a nutrition app that assists with meal tracking, portion control, and supporting you in your efforts to be healthy. You have tried multiple apps and they all are helpful, but none of them provide the exact solution you want.

You are looking for a nutrition app that pairs you with a partner who is just like you. Like dating but for platonic relationships for nutrition. The person can be anonymous and you share actual meals with one another down to the exact ingredients bought for making the meals. You can create groups if you like and belong to multiple groups at once or none at all, just like social media groups. You want a nutrition app for you, not for the generic masses that all of the other nutrition apps you have used were created for. Put simply, you want a tailored experience for you and you believe many others will want the same thing as you.

At this point, here are two critical items you just completed:

1) You identified an area, service, or idea that interests you to help solve an issue for customers.

2) You found a niche within that service or idea that is not being addressed by existing products to your knowledge.

For item number two, note that there is an old expression, "The Riches are in Niches." Like the law of large numbers described at the beginning of the book, this timeless expression will be as helpful years from now, as it was in the past. We will review niches more in Chapter 3: Within the boring niches, lie the real riches.

For now, know that the most important part of building your business is servicing needs that are unmet, or not fully addressed by others. These needs are typically found in niches that are so ordinary, that they were hiding in plain sight, yet no one has acted on them, until you came along. By the time others see them, you already have established your dominance in the niche and have a customer base.

# HOW BORING IS YOUR BUSINESS?

Now we must ask one more question before we complete the 5 Ws and 1 H. How boring is your business? Of course businesses don't have to be boring, but the more boring they are, the greater the chance your business will do very well for years to come without worrying about competition.

Businesses can have high barriers of entry stopping or slowing competitors from entering the field. Lack of glamor for a business is a barrier to entry that most don't talk about. After all, it's human nature to brag about yourself which includes what you do for a living. So who wants to brag about running a plain business? Therefore, the more boring your business, the greater the barrier that stops others from competing against you. The fewer competitors you have, the more time you have to establish and grow your business until you become an important player in your industry, if not a leader. Boring businesses are good.

To determine how boring your business idea is, ask yourself what kind of reaction you would get if you described your business to someone at a party? Would you be embarrassed to describe your business to anyone? What kind of reaction do you think a parent or relative would convey if they described your business at a party? Would a parent or relative even understand your business?

The less enthusiastic the reaction you receive from others when explaining your business the more boring it likely is. Of course you can be terrible at communicating, but the point is that if reactions to your business idea are "huh?" and "who cares?" yet you believe that it is a service or product which you and others would pay for, then congratulations, you have a boring business. Now, you can successfully grow it in the years to come.

## EXCITING BUSINESS IDEAS

Of course, it goes without saying that you can successfully grow glamorous businesses too. However, as mentioned earlier, the more barriers to entry that your business has, the fewer competitors you endure, thus increasing your probability of owning your market. In our example above a nutrition app has very well-funded and established competition. The chances of owning a market with competitors, especially established and well-funded ones is infinitesimal. What do you do?

As we'll explain more in Chapter 3: Within the Boring Niches, Lie the Real Riches, you find a niche which your competitors have not and cannot add to their platform easily. By doing so, you set your business up for success, even if you are in a competitive industry. To stack the odds in your favor even more to build an extraordinary business, make sure that the niche features and functionality you added to your product or service fulfills an unmet need in the marketplace to a defined target market with deep pockets.

A good rule to follow is that the more mundane your business is, the greater your chance of having limited to no competition. In fact, although it is not foolproof, having limited or few competitors is a good method to determine if you have identified a boring business. Conversely, the more exciting the business is, the greater the chance of having multiple competitors. This situation necessitates having a better defined niche market of customers to ensure that your business will succeed. Businesses that are more exciting also require quicker and nimbler execution since competitors will be ready to copy your ideas.

Put simply, it is far easier to create an extraordinary business in industries with fewer competitors. As true as this may be, it is your business that you are building and if you want to build it regardless of how many competitors there are, then build it. Just be aware of the additional challenges that come from making this decision.

A simple table below called the Extraordinary Business Table may help clarify where your business fits as it relates to the probability of creating an extraordinary business.

## EXTRAORDINARY BUSINESS TABLE

The boxes in green, on the left hand side of the Extraordinary Business table, offer the best probability of creating an extraordinary business, followed by the boxes in red on the right hand side. The bottom of the table has text descriptions referring to the number of competitors ranging from few to many, while the left side of the table has text descriptions referring to the target market ranging from niche to mass.

## ORDINARY STEPS FOR CREATING AN EXTRAORDINARILY BORING, NICHE BUSINESS

|  | Limited to Several Competitors | Many Competitors |
|---|---|---|
| Niche market with defined customer base | 1 | 4 |
|  | 2 | 5 |
| Mass market where everyone is a customer | 3 | 6 |

Following are descriptions of the business environment relating to each number shown in the Extraordinary Business Table.

1) Number one in the table represents the ideal type of business defined in this book. This is a business which has limited to several competitors which also targets a niche market with a defined customer base. Since the business appeals to a niche market, there are features and/or functionality provided specifically to the niche market increasing the probability that the business succeeds and may even own its market.

2) Number two represents a business which also has limited to several competitors. Unlike number one, number two offers their service or product to a larger audience to ensure staying ahead of competitors while earning enough to be successful. Offering products or services to a wider audience means that there must be a greater set of features and/or functionality since a wider

audience has more diverse needs, requiring the business to be more things to more people.

3) Number three represents a business which like numbers one and two has limited to several competitors. However, number three offers its product or service to a mass audience to be successful. Since a mass audience is extremely diverse with many needs, the business can respond by offering a generic service or product meant to please everyone. Additionally, at greater costs than numbers one or two, number three can provide a greater number of features and/or functionality to please the masses since it does not have many competitors.

4) Number four represents a business which has many competitors giving the business pause as to whether they can successfully offer the product or service to a niche audience and make enough money. Having multiple competitors' means that there might not be enough money from a niche or defined customer base to go around for all competitors. Identifying that your defined target market has cash to spend for your offering helps increase your probability of success in this environment.

5) Number five represents a business with many competitors necessitating a wider customer base to sell to. Unlike its counterparty, number two, number five must contend with so many competitors it is not clear whether the business can make enough money to support

itself while fending off the competition. The more competition, the better the product or service must be, which requires money, resources, time, patience, and luck. Tread carefully when creating a business in this type of environment.

6) Number six may be the worst of all business worlds as it represents a business which not only is saturated with competitors but is also focused on servicing a mass audience. Although not impossible, it is extremely difficult to be all things to all people with products or services when competing against many other businesses. Businesses in this environment must contend with the reality that the market does not necessarily want to buy another "me too" product or service in a crowded industry. Plus it may cost too much to build an offering that can be differentiated enough to please a mass audience. It is strongly advised to not create a business in this type of environment.

To increase your probability of success, consider how many competitors are in the industry of the business you are creating. Also, determine how defined and wealthy the audience you are marketing to is. The more competitors there are, the more defined your product or service should be to a well-funded market also known as your niche market. However, if the defined niche market is not big enough to support your company due to the number of competitors, you have some difficult decisions to make.

It is therefore recommended to focus on businesses in the green or left hand section of the table which enables you to create a business that is:

1) Mundane enough where you will likely have less competition but not so mundane that you do not have any customers.

2) Able to successfully support itself due to there not being too many competitors even when marketing to a mass audience with diverse needs.

3) Able to have more time and flexibility to be perfected as the less competition you have, the more you are able to experiment with your business line of products and services.

4) Increasing the probability of longevity or lasting until you no longer want to run the business. The longer you run your business, the greater your chance of it becoming extraordinary, which is how you gain independence and financial freedom.

Going back to our example of a nutrition app and applying it to the Extraordinary Business Table, we are initially disappointed to find out that we fall under business number four since there are many competitors with nutrition apps. Still, we do not let our discouragement stop us as we believe that if we focus on a niche market with a well-funded defined customer base, we can still succeed as a business.

We realize that we will likely require more resources and money to build our business due to many existing competitors. Additionally, we are prepared to execute our plans quickly to stave off competitors as we gain traction. The nutrition app is our passion regardless of the fact that it's not in the green area of the Extraordinary Business Table.

Knowing all of this prepares us for the next step in our process, answering the 5 Ws and 1 H. In fact, it may take days or even months to properly answer the 5 Ws and 1 H questions. Our market-based personas may change over time as more information is gathered. If so, GOOD! It means it is working. The more time you spend on answering these questions, the more defined your business is. These questions help develop a business plan.

## FIRST W: WHO

Who is the user of your service or product? Be as specific as possible and if there are multiple user types or personas, list them all.

1) Is your service primarily for:

   a) Males aged 20-29?

   b) Females aged 30-34?

   c) Both males and females, etc.?

   d) Demographics included in your target market:

   i) Age.

ii) Gender.

iii) Interests.

iv) Activities and hobbies.

v) Marital and family status (children or no children).

vi) Profession.

vii) Income/Financial Status.

viii) Living status (alone or with roommates or family).

ix) Location (city, suburbs, what country).

## SECOND W: WHAT

What is your service or product? Write down many details about your idea. Writing down your thoughts enables you to be more transparent with your ideas, strengths, and weaknesses. You may start with one thought and veer off into completely new territory. This is normal and to be expected as you continue to write about your "what." After you write down all thoughts on your idea, re-write your "what" in one simple paragraph and if possible even one sentence. Typically the less explanation that is required the more thought out the idea.

# THIRD W: WHEN

When will users or consumers interact with your business? Is your business transactional, subscription, or something else? Will consumers have an opportunity to interact with your business on an ongoing basis or is it one-and-done? Will consumers share your business with others or not? Each of the Ws offer opportunities to answer critical questions but "when" is easily ignored even though it offers some of the best problem solving ideas.

Let's say that your business interacts with consumers multiple times a day on a subscription basis such as with a health/nutrition app that tracks meals. Knowing when you interact with your users or consumers enables you to start thinking about partnerships with other apps or services that can be mutually beneficial.

For example, you want to grow users quickly while also controlling the user experience to ensure all bugs are resolved before you complete a wide rollout of your app. Within this example, a local coffee shop, which you frequent, offers healthy snacks and gets a decent number of customers each day. You approach the owner of the coffee shop and explain what you're creating with your business. You must be prepared for this meeting (see Chapter 4: Complete Your Business Plan, and Chapter 6: Sales & Marketing - Who Are You?). Ahead of the meeting, project how much new business you can bring to the coffee shop.

In the meeting, propose a joint venture of creating pre-programmed healthy snacks and meals in your app, based on food and drink availability for the coffee shop. Explain how the idea is a win/win as it offers you a value-added service for your local users, while expanding business for the coffee shop, especially for less-popular menu items.

The owner of the coffee shop agrees to display your app to customers in exchange for free advertising on your app as well as a percentage of revenue from each subscription sign-up their coffee shop provides as tracked with a special code provided to customers of the coffee shop. Congratulations, you just made your first big sale. Now, your well-funded and established competitors don't seem so scary. You may have found a niche in focusing on local markets. However, it's not time to get cocky as we have much more work to complete.

## FOURTH W: WHERE

Where will consumers and users interact with your business? Is there an online component to your business? Is interaction limited to one setting or multiple settings? For example, with the nutrition app, users will primarily interact online, using an app on their phones, fitness watches or laptops. Users are expected to enter data while in restaurants, coffee shops or their kitchens.

Similarly to answering the "when" question, the more details that are provided for answering where users interact with your business, the greater the chance that ideas will springboard which will assist with the sales, marketing, or product development aspects of your business. When you think about where your users will interact with your app, think about physical locations, or online areas, where you can see them frequently interacting with your app.

Let's say that you expect the majority of users to interact with your nutrition app in their kitchens for breakfast. Let's also say that you have determined that your primary target consumer is women aged 20-29. By completing the where question you realize that many users will be expected to interact with the app in their own kitchen for breakfast, allowing you to add relevant product features based on this information.

As you write down the different places you expect your users to interact with the app, you start developing other ideas. One idea that arises is providing daily fitness or health suggestions in your app based on your users' physical location. If some of your users are interacting with your app on their phone in the coffee shop, they may be willing to buy other products besides food and drink for their meal. You come up with an idea called "The Breakfast Bouquet" whereby you provide physical goods from the coffee shop, which becomes another revenue generator for you and another reason for your users to use your app. You start brainstorming what a breakfast bouquet item may look like and you come up with the following product description:

> Research shows that certain scents have a great effect on your senses. Today, try smelling peppermint before eating and coffee beans after. Buy our 'awaken the senses' breakfast bouquet for just $9.99 at The Coffee Shop or buy online by clicking this link and we will ship it to you.

Prior to answering the "where" question, you were only thinking of selling a nutrition app. Now your mind is racing as you realize that you can do all sorts of product offerings and partnerships that will grow your business. What if you do a subscription business instead, etc.?

Your creative juices continue to flow, as you think about ten other ideas out of seemingly nowhere, which is exactly why this exercise is so important to complete.

## FIFTH W: WHY

Why is a user or consumer using your business? Questions beginning with why tend to be annoying or not well received. Don't believe me? Spend a day asking why questions to everyone you interact with, or spend an afternoon with a toddler and answer every soul-sucking question you receive that begins with why.

Why are "why" questions annoying? Because "why" questions are the devil's advocate for everything. We all like to think of ourselves as bastions of greatness with excellent minds and virtuous actions. Why questions lay waste to that fantasy scenario. Answering enough "why" questions will leave you quaking in the corner of a dark room begging for relief.

Still, the more "why" questions you can answer, the stronger your business will be. For example, why will users use your nutrition app?

Well, you ponder, it will help them enter in all meals so they know that they're eating nutritiously and can reach their goals.

Very good says the devil's advocate in your head, but why would they use your app? After all, there are hundreds of available nutrition apps.

Well, you calmly answer the question, our app is the only one that is tailored to the female demographic who lives in coastal states and is single between the ages of 20-29. She earns well over 75k per year and cares primarily about maintaining her fitness goals.

Now your mental devil's advocate smiles and asks but why your app? You have not provided any details into why they would use your app instead of the multiple others out there. You may have your target user set but who cares? What are you offering to them to make them use your business?

You are no longer calm but you answer again and the wheels on the bus go round and round.

Is this mental courtroom battle between your business self and your devil's advocate self necessary? Yes, only if you want your business to be the best it can be. Do you want to be part of the very small percentage of business owners that not only succeed but grow their business to a valuation worth millions of dollars?

If so, it is strongly recommended that you have this mental conversation. Of course if you have any friends or relatives brave enough to take the role of devil's advocate, ask them for help. Just ask them to be brutally honest, but you cannot take anything personally. Nobody likes negativity, especially when it's not constructive but having everyone only tell you what you want to hear will get you and your business nowhere quick.

## ONE H: HOW - WELL, NOT QUITE YET...

How is the toughest of all the questions asked and requires bigger questions to be answered first. In fact, you can argue that these other questions should have been asked first but weren't. Why not?

Because like the annoying middle school math teacher you had, I wanted to show you a way to solve the problem first before I showed you the better solution. The five Ws are walking, while the one H, and its additional questions, are crawling because they help identify a business that suits you.

In the next chapter we answer the one H, "how" and the additional questions that determine the best type of business that suits you.

## CHAPTER 1 CHECKLIST

1) Identify what types of business ideas interest you.

2) Find an unexplored niche service or product within the scope of the business idea that interests you. The service or product should solve an issue or problem for you and/or others.

3) Determine how boring your business idea is by identifying how many competitors your business will have. The more boring the idea, the better as it typically means less competition. However, you can successfully create a more exciting business with more competitors as long as you have a strongly defined niche with a defined customer base willing to pay for your product or service.

4) Additionally, the more competitors you have the greater the probability that you will need more resources, funding, patience and quicker execution time to be successful. It is recommended, but not required, to stay within the sweet spot contained in the Extraordinary Business Table to create your successful business.

5) Answer the 5 Ws.

CHAPTER 2

# IDENTIFY A BUSINESS THAT SUITS YOU & ANSWERS YOUR 1 H - HOW

## CHILDHOOD

In my best psychologist's impression, I am now going to ask you about your childhood. This helps determine what type of business suits you best. Note that I say suits *you* best. You may be able to do many different types of businesses, but which of these suits you best?

In other words, like a marriage, which of these businesses can you stick with and be content with years down the road when the business does the spousal equivalent of snoring in bed and committing dozens of daily quirks?

Each business is as unique as a person, having its share of positives and negatives. Pick a business whose negatives you can tolerate and even grow to enjoy.

You may notice that I compare businesses to marriage quite a bit. This is no mistake. A business is a long term commitment, just like a marriage, or any committed relationship. This is why knowing yourself is so critical to knowing your "how." The type of business owner who will marry once and put the work into having a committed marriage, regardless of troubles, is likely well-suited to create and build a business over time.

Conversely, a person who disavows commitment or has been married multiple times likely will not be interested in running the same boring business for 20 years. Instead this person may be more interested in serially creating and selling businesses every few years.

Of course this is a generalization and exceptions abound as with everything in life, but knowing thyself can save a great deal of heartache with your business just like it can in your personal life. Here are some questions to answer which should help determine what type of business suits you best as well as how to structure, fund and manage it. Answering these questions as well as others in this chapter reveals your "how."

## KEY QUESTIONS TO ANSWER

1) Think back to your favorite moments in childhood:

    a) What were you doing?

    b) Were you alone? If not, who were you with?

    c) What made the memories so lasting and great?

    d) When do you recall these memories in your current life?

        i) What do you think triggers the recall of the memories?

2) Have any other accomplishments provided you with the same type of feeling as one of your favorite moments?

    a) If so, think carefully to determine what ties the two events together.

    b) If not, what have you ever done that brings you the closest to the feeling you recall from one of your favorite moments?

3) You are on your deathbed reflecting on your life. Outside of anything to do with friends and family, what accomplishments are you most proud of?

a) What do you regret not doing?

b) What do you wish you did sooner?

c) Did you make your intended mark on the world? Why or why not?

Answering the above questions should provide some direction into your types of interests. For example, if favorite memories include building model airplanes or baking desserts, the idea of selling tangible products may be better suited to you. However, if your favorite memories include making others laugh or enjoying themselves through acting, playing an instrument, or singing, providing a service may be more suited to your taste.

These exercises are not meant to provide a clear answer, but they are instrumental in beginning the process of clarity. Do not jump with both feet into a business without carefully assessing whether you want to do the business you are planning.

For those who believe the idea of the business is to make money, that may be true initially. However, in your seventh year of business you may find that you need more than just money to keep you satisfied and focused. Answering these questions brings you closer to determining what type of business may be best suited to you.

If no true ideas came from either of the above exercises, think about all of the books you read, movies you watched, or stories you have heard. What has stuck with you? Delving into the answers of these questions may help tease out whether a service or product suits you better.

Other questions that help you determine your business structure follow.

## PARTNERSHIPS

Are you a lone wolf? Do you like solo adventures or do you prefer collaboration? How fortunate we all are to live in an age where you can create an entire business with or without partners. If you are a lone wolf, you can hire contractors to complete discrete tasks where you need assistance. Conversely, you can bring in one or multiple partners to fill in any gaps you may have in your skill set.

There is no right answer here, BUT the guy who likes comparing everything to marriage has a point to make. If you have partners, it is just like a marriage.

Once you create a partnership, ensure that you have a clear understanding of the roles each partner will perform. Hire a lawyer and an accountant, the expensive ones are typically worth it, so ask around to find out who has a good reputation. Think about what happens if the business fails or succeeds or if you or one of your partners wants to leave the business. Good lawyers and accountants offer invaluable help with these situations.

If you are a lone wolf and prefer doing things on your own, think about the following:

1) How emotionally intelligent are you?

2) How do you handle adversity?

3) When you're trapped in the well of adversity and only have one phone call to make, who do you call?

4) What if you're trapped in the well of adversity on a daily basis for a year? Can you keep calling the same person and depend on them?

5) Are there contractors who can help you through all of the issues you have? Do you have enough money to pay the contractors if there are more issues that need attention than expected?

6) Would sweat, or work-based equity or having someone else perform work for a percentage of the company be a better solution, than paying hourly fees for completed work?

## MONEY, MONEY, MONEY

Some business owners can speak at length about purpose and making the world a better place without once mentioning money. If money is brought up as a key factor in starting a business, this type of business owner will scoff at the suggestion. Money is a factor they may say but low down in the list far behind other virtuous items.

As you convince yourself that these virtuous business owners are somehow different from the rest of us starting a business for financial freedom, you start noticing different things. Perhaps you see them drive away in a car that costs as much as the house you grew up in or they mention exotic vacation spots they have frequented. It is not that this type of business owner is necessarily a liar or even a showoff, although that is possible. This type of business owner has likely already made enough money, so money is not their primary motivator.

If you are starting your first business, it is likely that you are not in the position of our virtuous business owner. Therefore, if you come across business owners like this in your quest to start your business, soak up their advice to your heart's content. But realize that you are not in the same position as them.

Money may not be your primary motivator either, but you do need to make a living, so money is required for starting your business and on your path to financial freedom. How this money, known as seed money or seed capital, is first collected and subsequently allocated to your business is one of the most critical factors in determining the path your business takes.

If you borrow money from friends and family, guilt may prevent you from taking big risks for fear of losing the money. If you sell everything you own for seed capital, the burnout associated with it may be a journey you can't recover from. So what do you do? Just like at the beginning of this chapter's section, you think about what suits you best. I have seen businesses succeed and fail using many approaches. Which way of gathering seed money for your business suits you best?

Assuming you or a partner without seed money start the business, your primary options include a combination of or one of the following options:

# FUNDING OPTIONS

## 1) SELF, FRIENDS, OR FAMILY FUNDING

    a) Sell some valuables or max out your credit cards (please don't do this)!

        i) Have you ever heard of the endowment effect? Essentially it means that you likely place a higher value on your belongings than they are worth. The best way to find out what your belongings are worth is to put them up for sale. You will learn quickly that belongings are only worth what someone is willing to pay for them.

        ii) Realizing this fact leads many to max out their credit cards. Please don't do this either! There is always another option. Yes, I know that you saw all of those videos of people throwing caution to the wind and maxing out their credit cards and it worked out great for them. However a couple of things to consider:

    (1) It may work out great, but if it doesn't you have a very large loan to pay back as the interest rates on credit card debt is extremely high.

    (2) Additionally, if things don't work out, you can still sleep at night without a big headache.

  iii) If you have a home, you can refinance or take out a home equity loan. Depending on your circumstances this may be a good option.

b) Borrowing start-up capital from friends or family is an option that may be available to you. If you go this route just realize that the advice Shakespeare wrote in *Hamlet* is as relevant now as it was then: "Neither a borrower nor a lender be." The line is spoken by the character Polonius to his son Laertes to caution his son that the dynamic of money changes relationships very quickly.

  i) Borrowing or lending money from friends and family can result in strained or stronger relationships but things will likely be different from the point that money exchanges hands forward.

ii) Quality advice for folks taking this route include having a clearly written contract or agreement and a means of resolving disputes, should any arise. Sometimes lawyers and accountants are the best psychologists you will ever find as they will fix problems before they happen. Yes, they can be expensive but to paraphrase a line I heard recently, you pay for their advice one time rather than paying for it every day due to the heartache and headaches that come from bruised relationships with family and friends.

c) Be a superhero. By this I mean work on your business by night and a regular job or side gigs during the day. Doing so enables you to save money over time which will be invested into your business. Another benefit gained from taking this approach is that businesses take time to become better. By working on a business during nights and weekends, you free up your subconscious mind to think about improvements to your business during the day. Sometimes great ideas are just good ideas that have had enough time for improvements to be found. Plus, there is no need to borrow money from anyone, sell your valuables, or refinance your home.

## 2) BUSINESS LOAN/SELLING BUSINESS OWNERSHIP

a) Taking out a business loan offers one of the most straightforward paths to starting your business. The

Small Business Administration (SBA) is a governmental entity that offers lending options to banks or lenders to lend money to business owners. Depending on the size of your business and your experience an SBA loan may be a perfect fit.

Additionally, loan options are available from different types of companies looking for the next "thing" to invest in. You can search out private equity firms and business networking groups to find local investors that may be interested in having a conversation.

In my experience meetings are beneficial and you may find an option that works perfectly. For example, you may receive a loan that offers a better interest rate from a private equity investor in exchange for the right of first refusal for future funding needs. There may not be any free lunches, but there are many ways to distribute the cost of the lunch.

b) Another straightforward option is selling business ownership directly to a private equity or investment group. Depending on the idea and plans for execution, this option can provide you with quick capital and helpful advice in exchange for a large portion or majority of the business. At an investors' conference some years ago, I watched a presentation from two founders discuss their path to success. Their point was that you can have different approaches to making the same amount of money and they definitely got their point across by the end of the presentation. Both founders sold their businesses and made a similar amount of money when all was completed. However, there was a huge difference in their process of making their money.

## THE FOUNDER'S APPROACHES

The first founder started the presentation by explaining how he grew his business by procuring multiple funding rounds from venture capitalists. Each round of financing valued his company at a much larger amount than the last, culminating in the eventual sale of the business for a solid nine figure range (the selling amount was not provided).

The founder paused before continuing that of the large sum of money that the company sold for, he walked away with a much smaller amount in the low seven figures, which can be assumed to be one or two million dollars. Of course a couple of million dollars is nothing to scoff at but assuming his company sold for $200 million makes his portion seem meager in comparison.

This means that he spent years building a business where he initially owned 100% to a point where he sold the business for a fortune when he owned a mere 1% of his business.

The second founder continued the presentation by stating that he owned 100% of his business from inception until sale. He took out personal and business loans along the way and upon selling made the same net amount of money as the first founder. The presentation was done and each founder answered questions explaining how much they each enjoyed their business journey and would not have done anything differently.

The first founder noted that he had always wanted to grow a business much bigger than himself. He knew that to accomplish this task, he would need help and a lot of it. His purpose came from the growth of the company and knowing that he impacted the world.

The second founder wanted to have control of his business. He did not have anything negative to say about the first founder's approach, he just preferred to be in control on a daily basis for his business. The two founders traveled very different roads to end up at the same destination. However, they each traveled the road that they desired, which is why completing this chapter is so important. You must know if you are traveling the right road for you and if not, be aware of that fact as it may lead to some issues in the future.

The presentation was well done and the point received. There are many different paths to the same destination. My takeaway was a step that I have incorporated into every product and business I have built since. The business must suit you. Otherwise you may feel stuck, or worse, for years doing something that you do not enjoy or with pressure that you are not comfortable with. This is yet one more reminder of why it is so important to answer the five Ws and one H.

As you review this section of the chapter, which of these two founders are you most like?

If you are not like either of them, what do you prefer?

In other words, what business suits you and what structure and execution plan sits well with you. Not thinking about these things before you start your business is a mistake. It is understandable if you do not have detailed answers for each but the more you know thyself, the greater your chances of being successful, however you may define it.

For some, the idea of taking out personal or business loans or selling equity in exchange for money are not options they are comfortable with. If you are one of these people, read on.

## 3) ROYALTY/LICENSE/CREATIVE DEAL

To many, the movie "Star Wars[6]" is one of the most popular and entertaining movies of all time. The story, noted in this footnote[7], of how Star Wars' creator, George Lucas, made his fortune is even more entertaining. Lucas created a niche that at the time, was considered boring, at least to the movie studios and toy companies. Lucas' boring niche was keeping the rights to merchandise associated with the movie which did and still continues to earn much more money than the movies themselves.

As a young child when the first movie was released, I can attest that my parents did their part in helping Lucas's net worth. In fact, I still remember saving up for what felt like a year to buy a figurine of one of the characters called a Jawa. After playing with it for a week or so, I lost it, forever gone to the labyrinth recesses of my family's station wagon, never to be seen again. I just looked up the figurine and in its packaging it sells for nearly $2,000. Maybe I should have searched the station wagon a bit more carefully.

Lucas found a boring niche which incidentally spawned innumerable boring businesses that value, trade and work with things created from a make believe world from the Star Wars movie.

If the prior funding options do not work for you, perhaps finding a creative solution is the best approach. Rather than a business loan, you can provide a royalty or revenue share to a partner who helps, create, sell, market, or distribute your business product or service. In this situation, you retain complete control of your business and forgo a percentage or amount of the profits in exchange for the partner's assistance. Royalty deals can be date or product specific.

One example is providing a revenue share for all products a partner sells at a specific conference. Another example is offering a percentage of all profits for a product in perpetuity. Alternatively, you can have the partner sell the products or services and provide you with a revenue share or royalty with each sale. Products can also be licensed or crowd sourced, depending on which option suits you best. As with all other business and funding discussions, it is recommended to speak to an accountant and lawyer for assistance.

It is also recommended to make all royalty, licensing and revenue-share deals fair to all parties. If your royalty partner is trying to extract every last penny from you in your negotiations, RUN, don't walk away. Everyone has to make a living but life is too short to get involved with those that are always looking to get an edge over you.

There is rarely one right answer for a business regarding how to best fund but there is likely one right answer for you. There is also no rule saying you cannot use multiple approaches for funding over a period of time. For example, perhaps you self-fund your business until you grow it enough to prove it is feasible. Then you can secure a business loan until you grow it large enough to sell some equity in exchange for even more funding or expertise.

Just remember that the more parties who are involved with your business, the more opinions and advice you will receive. Rarely do people or businesses offer an investment of time and money without expecting to be at the table making critical business decisions. Even so called silent partners do not stay silent for long if a business is not executing!

# WHAT IS SUCCESS? WHAT IS FAILURE? WHAT'S FOR DINNER?

How you define success and consider failure are the last big points to make as it relates to your how.

My first job after graduating college coincided with email gaining prominence and popularity. Businesses were starting to use email and it was a bit of free for all in terms of what you would find in your inbox depending on the day. Among the desert of garbage emails consisting of chain emails and jokes, a gem would appear.

One such gem told the story of the fisherman from the tropics and the business consultant. Note that there are many versions of this story, typically tailored to the point a person is trying to make. In this version, a consultant is on vacation in the tropics watching a fisherman at sunset dock his boat after a long day. The consultant questions how much money the fisherman makes from his daily work as well as his process to catch the fish.

The fisherman notes that he catches enough fish to feed his family and sell fish for a small profit. The consultant immediately points out how productive the fisherman could be with just a few simple tweaks, and if the fisherman really worked hard and scaled his business, he could eventually own a company big enough to list on the stock market which would give him enough money for the rest of his life. The fisherman asked the consultant what he would do after making his millions and the consultant replied that the fisherman could retire and fish all day.

The story is trite and saccharin, yet the point hit me hard in my early 20s, and I had a two minute long existential crisis until my boss needed something ASAP. The story centers on the point that most of us avoid answering. What is success? The fisherman and consultant in the story have different definitions of success. The fisherman likely defines success as doing what you love each day as long as it fulfills your needs. The consultant likely defines success as having a combination of wealth, fame or fortune. There is no right answer, but not asking yourself the question is definitely a mistake.

Similarly, what are your thoughts on failure? Do you even use the word? Some refuse to use the word failure and instead mentally replace it with opportunity or experience. Others wear the word like a badge of honor and will be only too happy to tell you about how all their failures led or will lead to their ultimate success. Do not look to others for the definition of success or failure.

Answer the two aforementioned simple, yet complex questions yourself. Knowing what success and failure mean to you may be the difference between your future self feeling satisfied with life and feeling trapped on the merry-go-round of searching for purpose. If you do not know why you are doing something, how can you know when it's time to do something different?

Finally, have fun along the way. Enjoy the process of building your business. Years later when you look back at building your business, you will not remember the tough days or the fun days. Instead, in aggregate you will remember how it all made you feel. Go out to dinner, enjoy yourself a bit, the work can wait sometimes.

# CHAPTER 2 CHECKLIST

Realizing the importance of structuring your "how" as it relates to deciding on having partners, how to fund, how much runway you need to prove your business, and how to execute will save you much grief in the future.

When pursuing any of these options, always remember that like marriage, your choice of funding has life-altering and possibly long term implications. Get creative if you must, but do not wait indefinitely to start your business as there will never be a good time.

Following is a checklist of items to help you determine your "how:"

1) Answer questions in the chapter to determine what type of business suits you best.

2) Figure out which type of business structure makes the most sense for your business and personal needs.

3) Identify how you are funding your business.

4) Define what success and failure mean to you.

## CHAPTER 3
# WITHIN THE BORING NICHES, LIE THE REAL RICHES

You know how some are born with a silver spoon in their mouth? I wasn't and if you're reading this, I doubt you were either. We're the lucky ones. What, you ask? How exactly am I lucky for having less than others? The answer is simple. There are more of us than them; and you, being a part of us, see the world as the rest of "Us." This is your inside track. Use it to your advantage and follow these steps:

1) Put on your investigative reporter hat (5 Ws).

2) Figure out how to solve a problem for yourself by providing a product or service.

a) Boring areas that most don't care about are the best place to look.

   b) Profitably fulfilling niches within boring areas in scale optimizes your chance of lasting success.

3) Make sure that your business idea suits you and finalize your "How."

4) Build your business.

5) Execute your vision.

So if you were born with a low grade plastic spork in your mouth realize that you can use your unique talents and how you see the world to your advantage. This chapter focuses on how to find a boring niche and build a successful business to profit from it.

## HOW TO FIND A BORING NICHE?

To find a boring niche, first take an industry that interests you and try to find a unique product or service that derives from that industry. Preferably the unique product or service is a tiny subset of the industry. If the industry is clothing, the unique product may be a brightly colored sock. In other words it is a less important, less regarded subset of the industry where it belongs.

For our purposes of building a successful business without having to worry about a great number of competitors, we want to find a business that attracts less attention. Therefore, the more boring the business idea, the better. If you want to be on the cover of a magazine, I'm not your guy and this is not the book for you. Once you have your boring niche, the next step is determining the size of your industry, as well as how much of the market share you believe your business will be able to capture. Estimating how much revenue your business will make at launch as well as in the future helps push you forward on the journey of building your business.

## MARKET RESEARCH: TAM, SAM, SOM, AND THE BAND PLAYED ON

Once we have an idea of the industry we want our business to be a part of, we need to perform market research to determine the size of the industry and its associated customers. The size of the industry offers valuable insights into how profitable your business can eventually be. Identifying your customer base offers insight into how profitable your business will initially be. There are several different types of markets to research described below as well as in this article[8].

## TOTAL ADDRESSABLE MARKET (TAM)

Known as the Total Addressable Market, TAM assumes your business is a complete monopoly and owns the market for your product or service. TAM answers the question, if your business were the only one with your offering, what is the maximum amount you can earn?

## SERVICEABLE AVAILABLE MARKET (SAM)

Of course it is not realistic that your product or service will be bought by every conceivable customer in your market. This is why we also have SAM, or Serviceable Available Market. SAM adds realistic constraints to TAM such as location, online reach, and customer preferences. SAM answers the question, if your business were the only one with your offering in a specific location or that catered to a specific market, what is the maximum amount you can earn?

## SERVICEABLE OBTAINABLE MARKET (SOM)

As great as SAM is, it is still not realistic that every customer in your targeted market will buy your product. Enter SOM, or Serviceable Obtainable Market, which is also known as Share of Market. SOM provides a realistic estimate of how much of the SAM your business is likely to capture by adding key constraints including competition, logistics, and brand awareness. SOM answers the question, if my business were live right now, what percentage of the market would I realistically capture and how much revenue would I earn?

## EXAMPLE - MY IMAGINARY PIE BUSINESS

\* \* \* \* \*

In our example, let's say that my boring niche business idea is to sell pies that are healthier to eat for dessert. For my business I want to initially sell my pies locally and then eventually nationwide. I start by determining how much I can expect to make with this business. To do this, I start by searching online for articles about selling pies. I find several, including this one that points out that I can make six figures a year just by selling pies online[9].

However, I do not want to just sell pies from my house. I want to get investors for my business so I can eventually have a storefront and manufacturing facilities. If you were an investor would you invest in my company if my business research consisted of showing you an article that said I could make a good deal of money selling pies from my home online? What if I requested a large sum of money because I have big plans for my business? I tell you that I'm starting my business by selling pies locally, but I expect to also ship various food products all over our country and in time globally.

As an investor, you would likely ask to see a comprehensive business plan (see Chapter 5: How to Build Your Product or Service for more details), and provide many of the similar questions posed in this book to gain more information about my business. You may also ask more pointed questions surrounding how much my business could be worth and how I would execute my plan.

I understand your request and decide that I need to research and provide the industry size for my business. Since my business is pies and pies are contained within the food industry, I start by researching the size of the food market in the United States. As noted earlier in this chapter, the size of a market is known as the TAM, or total addressable market. I determine that the TAM for the food industry in the United States is worth about $1.5 trillion[10].

But, I am not just selling food. I am selling a specific subset of food, which are pies. Pies are technically food but for purposes of determining our TAM, it makes more sense to use baked desserts which are associated with bakery products. I dig deeper to determine the worth of the bakery products market. I find out that the TAM for the bakery products market is estimated to be worth over $450 billion[11]. However, this estimate includes commercial bakers and for now I want to sell my pies locally as a home-based retailer. I keep researching and find out that retail bakeries make about $3 billion per year with pies consisting of 2% of this revenue, or $60 million[12]. My TAM is now $60 million, which assumes that there are no competitors for my pies and every customer who wants a pie will buy one from my business.

Next, I determine the SAM which as noted earlier in this chapter, is the TAM with realistic constraints added such as location or brand awareness. Not everyone will know about my business as my brand awareness is limited and I wouldn't be able to make enough pies to supply every customer, even if it were possible. To determine my SAM, I research the worth of the bakery products market in my state, county, city and town.

Note that the local library has access to all of this information for free. You can visit the library and get help or use your library card to gain online access and find the information on your own.

Research like this is not always easy but that is part of the point. Easy is never going to be a word you will use in starting and running your business successfully. For researching about industries and markets, you can also join various sites for a fee that offer detailed industry-based information.

In our example, to determine the SAM, I visit my local library online and find out that there is a governmental code associated with my business's industry. The North American Industry Classification System[13] (NAICS) code for retail bakeries is 311811. I find a helpful industry report titled "United States Bread & Bakery Product Manufacturing Industry Report" that is free when using the library but costs $179[14] for purchasing.

With this report I identify that in my state, retail bakeries of all sizes make an estimated $500 million in total revenue. Small retail bakeries with between 1-4 employees make nearly $11 million out of the total $500 million in revenue. I happen to live in the largest city in my state and determine that about 90% of all revenue from my state is derived from my city, or nearly $10 million.

I decide that I do not need to provide county-based revenue estimates for my industry since my city comprises the majority of the revenue. I cannot find good information for my specific town so instead I explain in my business plan that my city is actually a metropolitan area comprising four equally large suburban cities. I divide the total revenue number of $10 million by four and estimate that the suburban city I live in has a SAM of $2.5 million. Note that my SAM value takes into account that my brand awareness will initially focus just on my suburban city. The SAM also assumes that I have no competitors and own the entire retail-based small pie market for my suburban city.

Now that I know my TAM and SAM, it's time to determine my SOM, or how much of the market I believe I can realistically capture. I think a bit more about my target market and decide that I want to focus on selling pies to working men and women between the ages of 25-55, who are looking for a sweet but healthier dessert pie to purchase at least once per week.

Utilizing demographic analysis that is shown in detail in Chapter 9, Business Optimization: Future Resistant, I determine that my SOM is between $250k and $500k. This means that including constraints such as competition, manufacturing, economic conditions, etc. I believe I can capture a respectable percentage of the market available to me.

To calculate the SOM percentage, I take the range of my SOM and divide it by the SAM. For example, the lower end of the SOM range is $250k while the SAM is valued at $2.5 million. $250,000/$2,500,000 is 10%. Therefore the lower range of the SOM I expect to capture is 10%. Repeating the steps for the upper end of the SOM range provides me with 20% of the market available to me or $500,000/$2,500,000. My SOM percentage is therefore between 10%-20%.

I am initially excited, mostly because I determined my TAM, SAM and SOM. However, my delight quickly fades once I realize that capturing an aggressive 20% of the market share provides a smaller amount of revenue than I had expected. When I've dreamt about my pie business over the years, I expected the numbers to be much bigger. The doubting questions start pouring forth:

1) *Can I actually capture 20% of the market (my SOM) or is my math off?*

2) *Even if I do capture 20% of the market, how much money will it take for me to accomplish this goal?*

3) *How profitable will my business be when all is said and done?*

4) *What do I do now?*

When these doubting questions appear, the smartest thing to do is take a deep breath and go outside for a bit. It is easy to get stressed out and doubt yourself. However, when you return from your break you may also begin to appreciate that the work you completed was helpful. After all, you found out quite a bit such as:

1) The total addressable market or TAM of my industry of retail pie goods needs to change from $1.5 trillion to $60 million.

2) The SAM, or serviceable available market, is $2.5 million.

3) The SOM, or serviceable obtainable market, has a value between $250k - $500k which equates to 10-20% of the market share available to my business when I go live. If I hadn't done this research and I walked into an investor meeting showing wildly inflated TAM, SAM, and SOM values, I doubt that I would be successful in securing investors as I was showing that I had not put much time and thought into my business research.

4) TAM, SAM, and SOM values are MUCH smaller than expected. The article I previously included noted that it's easy to make six figures selling baked goods and shipping them.

As you work through what you learned from the completed market research you may ponder questions such as should you change the business idea from selling locally to selling online? Questions such as these are important to explore as they lead you to other ideas. Continuing our pie example, as I think about selling pies online, I realize that when I researched competitors in the pie business, I did not see many bakeries selling healthy pies. My original idea for a pie-based business was to sell healthier pies but what if I forgot about healthier pies, and instead sold healthy pies?

Ideas such as these appear from the research you complete. In my example, I furiously start to scribble down the different types of healthy pies I could sell. None of the many bakeries I researched sold more than one or two healthier pies which did not look appetizing to me. The question keeps ringing in my brain, what if I just focused on selling healthy pies?

Next, I consult with friends and relatives in the medical field. I ascertain that my healthy pies are low-glycemic and fiber-rich, which are medically perfect for diabetics. In my original idea, I was planning on baking and selling pies locally. However, after completing some additional research, I realize that my business can move in multiple directions. I believe that I found my boring niche and possibly a perfect target market in diabetics and others with dietary issues, who cannot normally eat pies.

As I write down the additional work that's required, I realize that I must consult with a list of professionals including nutritionists, doctors, lawyers, and food scientists. Plus I have to try out new recipes and rework my SOM values. The work that I thought I was finishing led me to a path that was just beginning. A path to a niche that I'm defining and appears to be uncharted. I am resolute that I'll be ready for my investor meeting and my healthy pie business is going to take off.

\* \* \* \* \*

I wish the above example would work for everyone reading this book. How great life would be if you did not have to do the research or if you got it right the first time. However, good businesses take research, great businesses take re-tooling and excellent businesses take a never-ending process of exploration. As mentioned earlier in the book, there are no shortcuts to building an excellent business, but researching your markets (TAM, SAM, and SOM) offers a potential shortcut to identifying your boring niche. When done properly, your market research will lead you to some very important and interesting places where your markets may change as you refine your customer base and business offering.

There is an interesting point to mention when researching TAM for the industry you want your business to serve. It doesn't matter if you choose a large or small industry for your business as both can lead you to a successful outcome. If you choose a business in a large industry you have a greater chance of identifying a boring niche that can make your business profitable and unique. Conversely, if you choose a business with a small industry, you have a chance to own a larger segment of a niche market without having to worry about competitors jumping in.

Your goal as always remains independence through your business's success. That journey starts by you answering the following questions:

1) What is the TAM, SAM, and SOM for your product or service?

   a) Remember to be reasonable in determining your TAM, SAM, and SOM. Listing too many potential customers is a common mistake.

   b) Be brutally conservative in all of your estimates to gauge if you have a solid business. More information can be found related to calculating

TAM, SAM and SOM in Chapter 4. Complete Your Business Plan.

2) Would I use the product or service my business is planning on offering?

3) How much would I pay for the product or service my business is offering?

4) How often would I use the product or service my business is offering?

5) What is the cost estimate to create the product or service my business is offering?

   a) Estimates are best here. If you would use the niche product or service and pay decent money for it, you have an excellent starting point and should spend more time determining what the cost to it would be.

   b) Whether you are building a product or creating a service, your estimate is best determined by thinking through all of the components and steps that are necessary to complete your end result. Steps to complete this process are covered in more detail in Chapter 4. Complete Your Business Plan and Chapter 5. Build Your Product or Service.

6) Does anyone else provide the product or service my business is offering?

   a) If so, are they missing anything valuable?

b) Can I do it better or fill a hole in the marketplace?

7) Can others in the marketplace provide the product or service my business is offering just as well or better than me?

    a) Are there barriers to entry?

        i) How many barriers to entry are there?

        ii) How high are the barriers?

        iii) How many levers can be adjusted to manage competition to your business?

8) How valuable is my product or service?

    a) What value does it provide customers?

    b) Does it save time?

    c) Does it save money?

    d) Does it fulfill a need for your customers?

As demonstrated in Chapter 1: Be An Investigative News Reporter, product and service ideas are all around us and the more time spent delving into the ones that take a hold of you, the likelier you have found a good area to focus on.

There are dozens of ideas lying in wait for any area you can imagine. In the past few days of writing this chapter I heard about niche ideas for weddings, healthcare professionals and students. These are real businesses with one or dozens of employees:

1) Wedding: Service to help mothers of the bride or groom select the perfect dress.

2) Healthcare professionals: Software solutions to improve office management and learn new surgical procedures more efficiently.

3) K-12 Students: Tailored tutoring with parental takeaways to make the learning experience easier for child and parent.

Barring a viral breakout on social media, none of the above businesses will become household names. Yet, each of these businesses are providing valuable products or services to the marketplace.

The true miracle of capitalism is also its biggest failing, everything is there in front of you **IF** you know the process to follow. Do they teach the process to follow in schools? Not the schools we all attended, and likely not the ones we'd send our kids to either. So how do you learn the process to follow?

This is a perfect time to answer this question on how I learned this process. How did I go about finding a boring niche in an industry?

The quick answer to this question is that it all started with me refinancing my home. If you have ever bought or refinanced a home, you know the agony of waiting until everything is complete. There always seems to be one more step in a process that you urgently just want to be completed. Plus when interest rates are volatile you want to make sure that you lock in a good interest rate.

Today when you refinance there are free or lower cost options to lock in your interest rate. When I refinanced my home, locking in your interest rate was a steep extra cost that I didn't think was necessary. Oh how I learned the hard way that my sleep was more valuable than several hundred dollars as I laid awake at night wondering which rate we would get when everything was finalized. This thought process led me to wonder what was taking so long.

I questioned the mortgage broker who let me know that the delay was due to the bank. I questioned the bank and was told that it was my employer holding up the loan since my employment and income needed to be validated prior to approval. I questioned my employer who let me know that they outsourced the employment validation service and did not have any visibility into when it would be completed. I tried questioning the company that handled the employment validation but walked away without knowing when the process would be complete.

Meanwhile, I was watching interest rates vacillate on a daily basis. When rates plummeted I mentally got out the top hat, monocle and cane and pronounced loudly to nobody, as it was in my head, we will dine like kings tonight. On days when rates went up, which seemed to happen often, I mentally crawled into a fetal position mumbling to myself that I should have paid the extra money to lock the rate in and hoping tomorrow brought better news.

After a few weeks of this, I received the call that the process was complete. We ended the process with a decent mortgage rate - not the best, but not the worst either. The overall process shocked me though - how could it be so bad and how many companies were in this market? These questions led me to one overriding question: could I build a better proverbial mousetrap and improve upon this user experience? I believed that I could and it was then that I made the decision to do it.

I enlisted two former colleagues, an IT expert, and a Sales expert, and together we embarked on a journey to build a better mousetrap in this boring, niche industry. After years of struggle we succeeded in carving out a niche in the employment validation space.

## WHAT WAS OUR NICHE?

I noticed that segments of the marketplace seemed to be ignored as it related to employment validation. While employment validation may have been provided to these segments, it did not seem to offer a solution that catered to customers' true needs. Once determining the features and functionality that companies in the ignored segments wanted, it was easy to build our system around their needs. Ironically, many of our features and functionality became so popular that they were copied by our competition and thus became commonplace for all offerings in the industry. One more extraordinarily boring niche was created and the rest is history.

Throughout the process of creating your business, you may not know which things work without a great deal of trial and error. However, one great shortcut that you can take to reduce trial and error, is to enlist help.

This leads to the longer answer of how I went about the process of finding my niche and founding the business with my partners.

## ENLIST HELP - READ, LISTEN, WATCH, SOCIALIZE

There are many things that separate humans from other mammals but the one thing that makes us truly special is the ability to share knowledge over the passage of time. Other animals may be born with instinctual behavior to help with survival but humans are the only mammal that can share valuable knowledge from thousands of years ago.

It is estimated that over 100 billion people have lived on earth[15]. Knowledge that we all have today is because we stand on the shoulders of giants, or perhaps more importantly, saw what would happen if we did not stand on the shoulders of giants and ignored the important knowledge passed down over time.

Nursery rhymes, songs, poems, spoken words, books, quotes, sayings, acting, plays, movies, television, and social media are all remnants of our ancestors speaking to us from the past. There is a popular expression that you are the average of the company you keep. I say that we modify that expression to say that you are the average of the knowledge you intake. Where are you getting your knowledge from? Is it quality knowledge or is it junk knowledge? Just as eating junk food leads to poorer health, intaking junk knowledge leads to poorer outcomes.

For me, I was fortunate to have hard working parents that were raised in loving homes with parents who wanted a better life for them. My grandparents worked hard to help my parents have a better life and my parents paid the favor forward. My story is the living embodiment of the American dream. Great-grandparents with nothing to their names, came to America, helped their children, who attained more success and helped their children improve their station and so on.

I want to be clear there is nothing wrong with maintaining your station in life. In many ways, I believe my great grandparents were much happier than I am. However, this is a book meant to help with the steps necessary to start a business should you want to improve your station in life, if not through financial success, then independence from working for someone else.

I learned much from my parents, especially their mistakes, which they shared with my brother and me to help us understand and navigate the world. The knowledge I gained as I watched my father ascend in his career and handle ensuing layoffs to regroup and ascend again with his own business was invaluable.

Same for watching my mother work in multiple positions including starting her own successful business. Between speaking with my parents, watching them and other relatives and parents of friends, as well as reading, I had multiple lifetime's worth of knowledge when I was ready to start my business.

I am very fortunate that I had a dad who was a seasoned expert in designing and developing systems and by the time I was ready to start my business, I also had decades of experience of designing and managing systems. Between my dad and me, we had a very good idea of what works with systems and what doesn't as it relates to features and functionality. As an aside, I need to mention that even with our experience, there were still plenty of features that were expected to be well received but weren't as well as others that were demanded by nearly every one of our customers, which we hadn't thought of.

## HELP YOURSELF FIRST

Why am I telling you all of this? Because I am BEGGING you to enlist help in your quest to start and build your business. Help yourself first, through getting good knowledge sources but definitely enlist outside help. Following are several web sites that offer free courses on a seemingly unlimited series of topics.

If possible, go to a library and find music, books, magazines, movies and television shows that speak to your interests. If one of your choices doesn't spark something, try another one. You can also just go on social media to gain knowledge but be aware that you want quality knowledge, not junk knowledge.

Listen to a variety of sources and then distill the voices that best speak to you. The more knowledge you encounter the more lives you lead which enhances your ability to choose the life that you want.

**WEBSITES THAT OFFER FREE COURSES**

Khan Academy: https://www.khanacademy.org/
Coursera: https://www.coursera.org
edX: https://www.edx.org/

**CREATIVE SOURCES FOR HELP**

Help can come from surprising sources. As a child, one of my favorite memories is watching the concerts of the musician Harry Chapin[16]. Chapin gave free concerts often and through listening, I mean really listening to his music, I learned so much. He is best known for his song, "Cats in the Cradle," which I loved and still impacts me greatly in my life.

However, the songs that spoke to the child listening were "30,000 Pounds of Bananas," "What Made America Famous?," and "Six

String Orchestra." The simple lessons imparted to my little self by each of these songs: 1) Don't rush and be careful; 2) You can be one of the good guys too fighting for a better country and world; 3) A good team can make a not so good thing great.

My parents' *Verities & Balderdash* 8-track[17] is worn out from the number of times these songs were played after going to the concerts. What songs do you listen to that do this for you? How about books? How about movies, etc.? Get creative about the sources where you enlist your help.

As valuable as the above sources are, nothing is more valuable than people willing to lend a helping hand. Right now, there are people in your life that you know or can know who would be more than happy to help you, if asked.

These people can be family members, friends, neighbors or strangers you network with but they exist and they were once like you. Every person has a story to share. Maybe their story resonates with you and is helpful, or maybe you just share some nice time together.

The point being, enlist help! You don't have to take any advice you're offered, but the more you gather, the better informed your decision will be. Also, keep your eyes and ears open at all times. By doing so, you are learning, even if you're not aware of it.

# CHAPTER 3 CHECKLIST

1) Find your boring niche by identifying an industry that interests you and finding a unique product or service that derives from that industry.

2) Complete market research to determine the size of the industry and its associated customers. Market research includes:

   a) Total Addressable Market (TAM): Answers the question, if your business were the only one with your offering, what is the maximum amount you can earn?

   b) Serviceable Available Market (SAM): Answers the question, if your business were the only one with your offering in a specific location or that catered to a specific market, what is the maximum amount you can earn?

   c) Serviceable Obtainable Market or Share of Market (SOM): Answers the question, factoring in competition and the limits in your ability to market and deliver your product or service, how much would you earn if your business were live right now?

3) Answer questions in this chapter to refine your business idea.

4) Enlist help through your network of family, friends, acquaintances as well as books, music, movies, television and social media. Continue to learn as much as you can about your industry and never be afraid to ask for help.

# CHAPTER 4
# COMPLETE YOUR BUSINESS PLAN

The work we have completed thus far is integral to building a business plan. Some consider formal business plans to be outdated and unnecessary. There are valid points to why a formal business plan is not required, but if you cannot write a plan out, you may not understand your business idea as well as you think. Completing a business plan finalizes how well thought-out your idea is. Perhaps you have an excellent grasp when it comes to funding your company and building the service but you never thought about how to grow a customer base past your network of friends and family. So, is it necessary to write a business plan? Nope. But doing so enables you to think through different aspects of your business, increasing your likelihood of overall success.

There are many excellent resources online explaining everything you ever wanted to know about writing a business plan. I'm impressed by one in particular from the Small Business Administration's (SBA) site[18] and recommend it for completing this step. The SBA does a nice job of providing descriptions of each section. Following, are the traditional sections the SBA lists on their website, summary explanations for each section, as well as my commentary.

Note that the SBA also offers sample business plans for a product (wooden toys) and a service (consulting services). The sample business plans provide a baseline or starting point for developing your own plan. Also, the SBA recommends two different types of business plan formats, traditional and lean startup. I recommend completing a traditional business plan format first and then if you want to summarize further and convert to a lean startup plan, you can do so.

## BUSINESS PLAN SECTIONS

### EXECUTIVE SUMMARY

Provide an abridged version of the business plan that is easy to read and entertaining where possible. Explain why you are taking anyone's time to read the business plan. Your executive summary may need to be tailored to whomever is reviewing the business plan. You may want to highlight certain points to an investor while others to a potential business partner.

As noted, the SBA plans offer a baseline business plan. In my experience executive summaries are best received when they comprise a half to full page of the key information explained in the rest of the business plan. Put another way, an executive should be able to read the summary and understand your business journey. Think of the summary as a movie preview that upon watching makes you want to see the movie. You want the executive, investor, partner, etc. reviewing the executive summary to read about the intricacies of your business. Give them a good summary and they will read everything.

## COMPANY DESCRIPTION

The company description must answer key questions including:

1) What does your company do?

2) What problems is your company solving?

3) Who is your target market?

4) How is your company structured operationally and legally?

Providing general and detailed value propositions to all of your constituents (customers, partners, investors, and community) is strongly advised. You do not want to be all things to all people, but you must explain who your business is to each of your constituents along with the specific value you are providing.

Answering the questions from the prior chapters should make completing the business plan much easier as you've had time to think about your business from many different angles.

Completing your business plan is no time for modesty. Granted, you do not have to brag about anything and everything but provide specific brief examples in this section as to why you and your team offer the best product or service as opposed to your competitors.

## MARKET ANALYSIS

A good market analysis shows that you understand your industry well. Answering questions from earlier chapters helps here as well. Provide more detailed answers to why your business is the best choice out there as opposed to your competitors. Explain what you believe the future market will look like, after your business enters the industry. How will you change the market and what will you do if your competitors match your competitive advantages?

As noted in Chapter 3. Within the Boring Niches, Lie the Real Riches, ensure that you provide reasonable estimates for each of your markets (TAM, SAM, and SOM). There are various ways to calculate your estimated markets, and the brutal truth is, the most commonly used approach is the one that makes your business look the best for investors.

Make sure that you address the questions that your investors will be asking. This includes details on what your market research is focusing on as well as how you calculated your estimates. Otherwise you risk losing credibility with meaningless claims that there is a $100 billion dollar addressable market for sneakers so your customized laces will easily make $1 billion since you conservatively plan to capture 1% of the total market. The more conservative your estimate, the greater your chances of landing investors, partners, employees, and customers.

As noted in the company description section, brag! Explain how well you know your target market and what the market will and will not accept from you or your competitors. The market research in the SBA example for Wooden Grain Toy Company did an excellent job of showing that they understand their market. Be as detailed as possible.

Some shy away from showing their "secret sauce" in business plans out of fear that others will steal ideas. This is always a possibility and a Non-Disclosure Agreement (NDA) can be as flimsy as an umbrella in a windstorm when needed. So, what do you do? I suggest providing enough detailed information to explain what you will do differently without providing the project schedule or plan of how your milestones will be reached. Worrying excessively about ideas being taken is a sure way to drive yourself crazy while taking up valuable time you could spend on building your business. This doesn't mean trusting everyone and being as open as possible with your great ideas; be judicious and share enough details without giving everything away.

Make sure to also include business risks to your plans such as competitors, economic conditions, and supply chain or resource issues. If you are looking for investors, include details in this section of the business plan on how you are mitigating risks.

## WHY NOT YOUR COMPETITION?

In Chapter 2: Identify a Business that Suits You & Answer your 1 H - How, we determined why consumers would use your business. In Chapter 3: Within the Boring Niches, Lie the Real Riches we delved deeper to gauge if there is active or potential competition to your business as well as get to the heart of the value of your business. This included determining its TAM, SAM, and SOM as well as answering questions. Now we must dig even deeper into our market analysis to state our case for why customers won't use your competitors' business.

Note the mental shift necessary from asking why customers would use your business to why customers won't use your competitors business. The answers to these different questions offer possibly extremely valuable insight into new features, functionality or services you can provide to optimize your business. As with the prior questions, the more well thought out and detailed the answers are, the higher the probability you have a great business idea on your hands.

Similarly, if you cannot construct answers to defend your business's life, it doesn't mean that you don't have a successful business, it just means that you may not be able to withstand current or future competition.

The point to answering all of the questions before building your business is to dispel magical thinking, the bane of business owners everywhere. The world is littered with big and small businesses run by people using magical thinking. Magical thinkers are people who assume business will always be good, competition will never succeed and should a problem arise, they proclaim loudly, "I'll figure it out like I always do." Perhaps they will. But like the saying goes, "Prepare for the worst, hope for the best." Otherwise, you run the risk of being like many in the business world who have failed startups that built a better mousetrap only to find out that the old mousetrap worked just fine for most consumers.

If you find yourself answering any questions surrounding why customers won't use your competitors with statements such as, "Our product has a better user interface or experience" take a step back and think about your answer more carefully. Although everyone prefers a better user interface or experience it is likely not enough to make anyone change services.

Think about all of the legacy businesses or systems you interact with that have sub-par systems. Without naming names, how helpful is your bank's mobile app or website? Is it better than the brand new fintech company sites? Probably not, yet you and nearly everyone else hasn't replaced your bank with the new fintech company's product. There are many reasons why you haven't left your bank, regardless of how poor their user interface or experience may be.

I have built, led, or been part of teams responsible for dozens of software products including home-grown systems, Enterprise Resource Planning systems, and Suite of Business Solutions. In all of these cases customer selection was never driven by user interface or experience. It may have been a consideration but it was never a driving force in a business decision.

In my experience, outside of political or influence-driven decisions, when determining which product or service to utilize, customers focus largely on several key items in descending order of importance. I call these items a "Hierarchy of Business Differentiators."

**HIERARCHY OF BUSINESS DIFFERENTIATORS**

1) Solving a Problem:

   There's that expression, "Give a person a fish and they eat for a day; teach them to fish and feed them for life." Solving problems brings to mind a different kind of quote: "Solve a problem for someone and you have a customer, solve multiple problems for them and you have customers for life."

2) Price of Product or Service:

   Customers care quite a bit about the overall cost of the product or service you and your competitors provide. Pricing also may be one of the easiest things for your competitors to change. In fact, if your competitors need to juice sales a bit, they may match or beat any price offer you have. If your competitors are well financed, they can also offer bundled services or product offerings, which easily negates your price benefit.

So, what do you do? You think carefully about bundles or promotions you can offer, which would be difficult, if not impossible, for your competitors to match. If you run your business efficiently, one big benefit you have is you can dynamically modify your business model. If your competitors are established it is likely that modifying their business model is extremely difficult and adjusting it several times per year is near impossible.

3) Convenience:

On paper, people will tell you that convenience is highly valued. However, in practice, price tends to matter more. If your business provides items one, two, or three in the hierarchy of business differentiators, you will likely catch lightning in a bottle.

4) The Little Things:

The little things include nearly every other reason why you think someone would use your business from product features to additional service offerings.

With more thought provided into our business differentiators, we can answer the following questions:

1) Why won't customers use your competitors' business?

    If you have a business that does not have any competitors, pretend you do have one and imagine how they would structure their business to compete with your business.

2) What problems are your competitors solving for customers?

3) What problems are your competitors NOT solving for customers?

4) How flexible are your competitors' pricing?

5) Do competitors offer bundles or anything that ties the customer to your business?

6) What is wrong with your competitors' pricing which stops customers from using them?

7) Where do your competitors fall short in being convenient for customers?

8) How difficult would it be for your competitors to fix any convenience issues?

9) How will your competitors sell against your business?

10) Are your competitors selling points against your company valid?

11) What can you do to insulate your business from the points your competitors bring up?

12) What else are you missing?

> There are always other points being missed about your competitors or understanding of your customers. Think deeply about items that you may have missed about your competitors.

The point of this exercise in asking, "Why not your competition?" is to have you think carefully about the features, functionality, and service offerings it would take to get customers to buy the product or service your business is selling. If you do not have compelling reasons, I suggest going back to the drawing board or finding another niche.

Time is too precious to spend building a product that is not addressing a market need which will capture enough customers to retain and grow a business. If you have not yet found your niche that is fine. Keep looking. It will come. After all, once your eyes are open to opportunities, it is impossible not to see them everywhere you look.

## ORGANIZATION AND MANAGEMENT

Before filling out this section, make sure to have a conversation with your legal and accounting representatives. The long term consequences to the decisions you make at the founding of your company cannot be overstated!

Once you structure your company, there are legal, accounting, operational, and mental health-related ramifications. Changes can always be made but as you grow your business it becomes more onerous to make changes. It's never impossible, just more expensive, time consuming and mentally taxing.

Find good representatives to help you and think carefully about how best to structure the operational structure of your business. Do not allow questions to be answered with gems such as, "We'll figure it out as we go along" or, "We'll find someone to do it when the time is right." These are famous last words of failed businesses OR partnerships that will turn sour over time.

Every single business that I am aware of, including ones that I have been a part of, have suffered greatly from leaving questions unanswered. Protect the future self of you and your partners, investors, etc. and answer all questions before the business is live.

In this section you can also add an operational model explaining how staff will manage the business on an ongoing basis. If you are seeking outside investors, include staff that you will need for your first day of business as well as for multiple years. Use placeholders where applicable for staff you know you will need to add in the future. If consultants are being used, make sure to differentiate between staff members who are employed, vs. staff members who are consultants.

## SERVICE OR PRODUCT LINE

This section answers the questions, what does your business do and how do you make money? The sample business plans offered by the SBA provided rudimentary information in this section. I suggest adding more detailed information on your revenue and cost model. Specify that the financial projection section of your business plan contains detailed figures and provide summary financial information in this section. The SBA does offer a calculator which you can utilize to better calculate your startup costs[19].

If your business model calls for a multi-phased build out, detail the primary objectives for each phase. It is common for new businesses to have a phased approach whereby primary objectives must be met first.

Explaining the order in which objectives are expected to occur, per phase, shows careful analysis and planning. Answering questions from prior chapters will help here as well.

## MARKETING AND SALES

Consider this section the prize of the business plan and also a challenging one to complete. Answering the following questions should help you complete this section:

1) How are you going to grow your business through sales?

2) How are customers going to find out about your business through marketing?

3) How are you making your revenue?

4) Are your sales transactional, on a subscription basis, from service fees or a mixture?

5) Do your customers make repeat purchases?

6) Do customers provide word of mouth about your product or service?

7) How are you planning on growing in your first year and from years two through five?

8) Who are your primary customers, vendors, partners and contractors?

9) What are the backup plans if your business is not growing the way you envisioned?

10) How long is your sales cycle?

11) How quickly do you receive revenue after a sale?

12) How much does each sale cost your business?

13) How many sales do you require to pay for each employee and support the business on an ongoing basis?

14) Do you have a website?

15) How important is your website to your business?

16) What is your marketing plan?

17) Do you have an online presence on specific or multiple social media sites?

18) Do you primarily use video, images or writing to engage your constituents?

19) Can you sell your product or service before delivering it to customers?

   For example, if you are a consulting company, can you receive half your payment upfront and the other half after your engagement is complete? If you are providing a product, can you receive payment up front and deliver the product on a future date? What happens if the engagement is never completed or the product never provided?

20) What is your customer retention strategy?

21) How are you receiving customer feedback?

22) How quickly can you make changes to your product or service based on customer feedback?

23) How are you and your staff directly engaging friends, family and social media to get the word out about your business?

## FUNDING REQUEST

Funding requests fall under the same critical category as legal, accounting and operational structure. Once you make a decision on funding, it is not easy to change direction. For example, if you fund with debt, you now owe money to a creditor that may make demands to your business at an inopportune time. Funding with equity may lead to restrictions on future direction as well. What do you do? Take the advice from prior chapters and think carefully about whether you want funding. If you want funding, determine what type by researching which method suits you and your business the best.

A proper funding request will show that you have completed your homework. If you are looking for a loan, specify the terms and make sure to provide a win/win for you and the investor. As mentioned earlier there are creative methods to accomplish this task. Include all details on how the funding will be used. Clarify rules of engagement with your lender to avoid unnecessary issues in day-to-day management of the business. Point investors to your strategic direction and plans for your business over the next three to five years. Finally, specify how you expect the business to conclude. For example, do you expect to sell the business within ten years, exit as CEO but remain on the board in five years or keep the business going as a family concern, where your children or relatives take over?

## FINANCIAL PROJECTIONS

Provide three to five years of financial projections, which include a breakdown of your revenue as well as expenses per year. Include the information provided below. Note that there are many financial model templates you can find online. Referenced here[20] is a link to a sample financial projection from the SBA:

1) How much are you going to charge customers for your products or service?

2) Do you charge customers on a transactional basis, by contract, product or finishing of work? Explain how your revenue is derived.

3) How much will running your business cost?

4) What is your net income?

5) What is your minimum level of profitability?

6) What does optimized profitability look like?

7) How do your projections compare to your competition?

8) When do you expect your business to become self-sustaining (enough revenue is received to support your expenses)?

9) Include the number of years and months until expected profitability. Also include how much capital you expect to need before your business earns any revenue.

10) If you are using an accounting-based system, bookkeeper or small business payroll system, generate all applicable reports. This includes income statements and balance sheets as well as any other pertinent information such as whether additional funding will be required and how that funding can be attained.

## APPENDIX

All supporting documents, spreadsheets and information required to complete this business plan should be provided as appendices in this section.

## CHAPTER 4 CHECKLIST

1) Complete each section of the business plan using answers to questions from the current and prior chapters for help.

2) In the market analysis section of the business plan, provide details on why your business is the right choice for customers as well as why customers do not want to use products or services from your competitors.

3) Determine how many differentiators contained within the hierarchy of business differentiators your business is providing. If you are not at least providing one key differentiator, more thought may need to go into your business, or you may need to explore a different business idea.

## CHAPTER 5
# HOW TO BUILD YOUR PRODUCT OR SERVICE

This chapter assumes that you have completed the work contained in prior chapters and have finalized your team and financing. Now it is time to start building your business.

First off, CONGRATULATIONS! It is not easy to make it this far. It is easy to have visions of what your business *would* look like, *if only*. The "if onlys" are what get us in trouble. It is never a good time to start a business or try something new until of course it is. You have made it past the "if onlys" to this stage, continue on and execute the plan. Let's build!

# INPUT ===> THROUGHPUT ===> OUTPUT

An exercise that may be helpful when building is to take a step back and think about the process that your product or service follows from inception to delivery. This exercise helps put into concrete terms the steps required to create and deliver your product or service.

## INPUTS

What do you need to create your end product? If you are manufacturing a product you need raw materials, instruments and equipment to manipulate the raw materials and tools to fine-tune the product. If you are designing a physical or software product to be built by others, you need to detail the specifications for the product to be built.

As you envision what you need to create your end product, you will likely begin to think of items that you previously had not considered. Begin this process by thinking about the journey each of your customers, employees, partners, etc. takes through your business process.

If you are manufacturing a widget, you may find out that one of the inputs of raw material can only be bought in bulk. If you find out that the input in question is available but only in a quantity that would last you a year, what should you do? Should you buy equal amounts of other raw materials that last you a year? If so, where will you leave the extra materials since your garage is already full? Do you need to get an outside workspace?

How about if you're outsourcing development of your software product? To ensure your requirements are complete, imagine the journey each of your users must take through your system. Some questions to answer which will help this process:

1) What are all the different ways a user can find out about your product? For example, online searches, links through social media, friends, etc.

2) How can users interact with your system? For example, online, phone, mail, etc.

3) How are users on-boarded through your system?

   a) Is the experience a pleasant one that you yourself would appreciate or is it lacking?

   b) What can be done to improve the process? Your customers' or users' journey must be your journey too if you wish to build a business that will stand the test of time.

Service companies can use this exercise as well. Once determining inputs, a service company can walk through an engagement process by answering the following questions:

1) How are clients identified, and sold?

2) How much work, if any, is completed prior to a committed engagement?

3) How is the ongoing interaction with the client managed?

4) How many employees from your business does the client interact with?

## THROUGHPUT

The business journey which transforms inputs into output is throughput. For manufacturing businesses, it includes converting inputs into the end product. For service businesses, it is performing the service for your customer. For software-based businesses, it can be taking an order or collecting information from a user prior to generating a result. Throughput consists of use cases, or specific situations in which your business's product or service may be used.

As with inputs, think about the steps involved in the throughput journey. Let's say your business is a service that walks dogs for customers. The throughput journey is determining what it looks like if you have five service orders to walk dogs at the same time, but only two available staff members. Additionally, in this use case, two of the service orders are for dogs which must be walked alone. How will you handle this situation?

Take the most common situations you can think of for your business and determine how you, your users, and customers interact in those cases. Completing this exercise brings about other items you did not think about when putting an initial list of requirements together.

It is advised to not be a perfectionist in this process, expecting 100% of all potential issues to be solved before you build your business. However, this does not mean you should ignore this process either, as putting the work in will help you with solutions to future issues that seem to appear out of nowhere.

Having good solutions for at least half the problems thrown your business's way, leads to a high probability that your business will do well. Plus as you run your business on an ongoing basis, you will quickly gain solutions to handle the remaining situations which appear. When uncommon situations occur, take a deep breath and remember that you are where you are because you have skills and are developing a product or service which customers want. There is not a problem that you cannot solve. If you need help, friends, family and the kindly mentor who was exactly where you are now 20 years ago, are on stand-by to help. You just have to ask.

## OUTPUT

What does the end result or product look like? If you are a Software as a Service (SaaS) business, and the end result is a report generated for the customer, several questions must be answered including:

1) What happens after the report is generated?

2) Can the customer download or share the report?

3) Will the customer be able to access the report in the future? For how long?

4) What is the cost of the one-time generated report? Is the cost based on each report the user generates or a subscription fee?

5) Will generated reports be updated for the customer if information changes in the future?

6) After the report or output is provided, what does the customer or user experience look like?

7) Do you request testimonials or service ratings? How do you interact with customers and other constituents from this point forward? For example, do you bombard users with emails daily or not contact them at all?

Note that your product or service may stop at the output stage but your business doesn't. Answering the above questions helps create a discrete on-boarding and off-boarding process for each user that interacts with your business. Think of a customer interaction with your business from beginning to end as a journey through your business. Make sure that you take the same journey through your business as your customers, partners and any other user. By doing so, you can improve any deficiencies you find along the way.

I once met a pilot in my travels who told me that an old trick that pilots used when arriving late is to say things such as, "We're a little bit behind schedule" or "We're coming in around our scheduled time." He said that by doing this, few people realized that they arrived late. Instead people remembered that their flight was about on time. The pilot said that it left a pleasant memory in people's minds.

It is the same concept with the off-boarding process. In cases where users or customers are not completely happy with the entire journey through your business process, providing a good off-boarding experience may make the difference in getting repeat business.

## PROJECT SCHEDULE/CHECKLIST

One of the reasons why so much time needs to be spent on the analysis and design of your business is that is where the success happens. Talk to an experienced realtor and they will tell you that your profit is made when you buy a home, assuming you got a good price. It is the same with business, assuming you put good work in, your business is already successful. You just have to wait for the results to show up.

A helpful tip to complete a project, be it small or big, is to break it down into smaller tasks or activities, and complete each of those tasks as appropriate. In other words, create a checklist. If your project is complex, use a project schedule. Many tools exist to help users or teams complete projects on a task-by-task basis, but for smaller businesses using a spreadsheet may work just fine.

Let's say that you have a team of contractors building a software product, and you want to showcase your progress to investors. To accomplish this, you may decide to create a working prototype. In fact, depending on the terms in your agreement with investors, you may have to complete a milestone such as "working system prototype" before receiving new infusions of cash.

In this example, to ensure that all parties are aligned, you decide to create a basic project schedule surrounding the work which must be completed to build a working prototype of your product. Doing so, lets all parties know which work activities are being completed at what time.

Using the sample project schedule below, you may have certain sales and marketing work activities that must be completed at the same time as system testing-based scripts to ensure that the system operates correctly before the prototype is live. All of these work activities may be completed together as a way of showing your investors the efficiency and dedication of your team.

Once the prototype schedule is completed, you can create a new schedule or checklist for the next milestone.

# SAMPLE PROJECT SCHEDULE - BUILD PROTOTYPE

| Task | Task Owner | Duration | Start | End |
|---|---|---|---|---|
| Analysis & Design | Contractor 1 JS; Team | 22 Days | | |
| Review Industry Requirements | JS | 6 | TBD | TBD |
| Complete reviews with business stakeholders | MJ | 4 | TBD | TBD |
| Finalize System Design | MJ | 12 | TBD | TBD |
| Requirements Discovery Completion | PA | 4 | TBD | TBD |
| Design Requirements Sign-off | Team | 1 | TBD | TBD |

| Program Development | Contractor \| JS | 30 Days | | |
|---|---|---|---|---|
| Development | JS | 22 | TBD | TBD |
| Unit Testing | JS | 7 | TBD | TBD |
| Development Completion (sign-off) | JS | 1 | TBD | TBD |
| Sales and Marketing | Contractor \| AC | 18 Days | | |
| Develop Marketing Materials | AC | 10 | TBD | TBD |
| Acquire Interested Prospect List | AC | 1 | TBD | TBD |
| Design "Coming Soon" Email Campaign | AC | 3 | TBD | TBD |
| Prepare email campaign | AC | 3 | TBD | TBD |
| Execute email campaign | AC | 1 | TBD | TBD |

| Testing/Quality Assurance (QA) | BM | 8 Days | | |
|---|---|---|---|---|
| Iterative System Testing (stress/volume/functional) | BM | 4 | TBD | TBD |
| QA Completion (development fixes and re-test) | BM | 3 | TBD | TBD |
| QA sign off | BM | 1 | TBD | TBD |
| User Acceptance Testing | FA | 5 Days | | |
| Complete Test Cases | FA | 3 | TBD | TBD |
| Sign off | FA | 1 | TBD | TBD |
| Go-Live | FA | 1 | TBD | TBD |

How about if instead of creating a project schedule, you decide to use a checklist on your Notes app on your phone? That's possible too. You are the business owner and get to decide how to structure your business. As long as you make sure that the work is being completed, you can use any approach that works for you.

Following are sample tasks that a service-based company may have from the initial sales meeting through engagement completion. These tasks can be entered into a task management system or even notes.

## SAMPLE SCHEDULE FOR CONSULTATIVE SERVICE BUSINESS

1) **Sales Meeting**

    a) Present Engagement Proposal:

        i) Value Proposition.

        ii) Expected Cost Savings.

        iii) Pricing (tiered by cost savings).

        iv) Proposed Engagement Responsibility Matrix.

2) **Client Acceptance**

    a) New Client Information Request Form.

    b) Client Onboarding (internal):

        i) New Account Creation.

        ii) Service Offering Confirmation.

        iii) Account Manager Selection.

        iv) Set Meeting to Confirm Next Steps.

        v) Send Official Engagement Letter.

3) **Engagement**

   a) Complete Requirement Analysis.

   b) Analyze Client-Provided Data Files.

4) **Design Customized Process**

   a) Form Collection Reduction.

   b) Modify Escalation Process.

   c) Re-tool Certification and Follow Up Process.

   d) Verification of Opportunity Analysis.

5) **Deliverables**

   a) Revised System Process.

   b) Sample Revised Data Files and Collection Process.

   c) Industry Best Practices List.

   d) Success Probability Factor Matrix.

6) **Client Presentation**

   a) Delivery of Work Products.

   b) Client Acceptance.

7) **Engagement Completion**

   a) Invoice Issued with tiered savings confirmation.

   b) Future discounted work if requested within two months of payment receipt.

   c) Survey.

      d) Testimonial.

8) **Maintenance**

      a) Ongoing Follow-up.

# STARTING A COMPANY - BASIC NEEDS

Don't forget about all of the "little things" involved in building your product or service. Namely all the common items all businesses require for their customers, employees and partners. Your specific needs will vary so as with other items from this book, check with your legal and accounting advisors for assistance:

1) Identification Numbers: Just as citizens of a country have a unique identifier, such as a Social Security Number in the US, companies are required to have Federal and state-based Identification Numbers for tax purposes.

    a) Register with the IRS, using the footnoted link, for your Federal Entity Identification Number (EIN)[21].

    b) Register with your state, using the footnoted link, for a state-based Identification number[22].

2) Agreements and Policies: Depending on your circumstances, some agreements may be required prior to forming your business while others can wait until they are needed. Typical agreements and policies include the following:

a) Operating agreement: Required for certain business structures such as Limited Liability Corporations. An operating agreement provides details on many items including, ownership terms, roles and responsibilities of each member and rules for how the company will be governed.

b) Partnership agreements: Highly recommended for any partnership or investor relationships as the agreement includes detailed provisions on buy/sell agreements related to ownership of the business. Similar to an operating agreement, partnership agreements can also provide clear lines of direction and management of the company.

c) Employment agreements: An agreement that contains pertinent information surrounding employment expectations. Consider this agreement to be the ground rules for employment at your company.

d) Non-disclosure agreements (NDA): An agreement between your business and employees, or other parties that protects sensitive information from being shared by either party.

e) Non-compete agreement: Non-compete agreements are meant to protect employers from competition from former employees or partners that have valuable business knowledge surrounding the company. However, non-competes have become a politically sensitive topic as they have been taken to an extreme by some industries. As with all of the other agreements, discuss the merit of using a non-compete agreement to determine if it makes sense for your business.

f) Employee Handbook: Provision of guidelines and rules for the company. Once you have enough employees that there are questions surrounding why Joe gets to work from home three times a week but Sally can't, it's time for an employee handbook so rules are applied evenly and understood by all.

g) Privacy Policy (Terms of Service): Policy that states how data is utilized by your business, including customer data, employee data and partner data. This policy is typically front and center on your corporate website and in the employee handbook for employees.

h) Terms and Conditions (T&C): T&C's are a contractual relationship between your business and users of your system. Other common names for T&C's are terms of service for service providers and End User Licensing Agreement for software providers. T&C's can be many pages long containing a catch-all of various terms and conditions regarding use of a system, service, or product.

3) Compensation

a) Base Pay: Determining base pay is simple for your first employee and possibly even employees 2, 3 and

4. However, as you continue to grow you may regret not putting more thought into the compensation package for your employees. Some employees may value flexible or static hours in exchange for lower base pay. If that enables you to invest more in the company, or extend your timeframe for profitability it may be a good decision. Base pay is only one factor in compensation and must be weighed with the other factors in mind.

b) Bonus: Just as with base pay, bonuses are simple at first but can get complicated very quickly. Some businesses use a Special Performance Incentive Fund (SPIF) to payout contributions on an ongoing basis. Other businesses use an annual bonus based on individual or group performance. Still others use a combination of bonuses to continually incentivize employees.

c) Restricted Stock Unit (RSU): An RSU is a form of equity or stock ownership in your company, provided to employees who must meet certain conditions before receiving the stock. Conditions can include performance-based goals, business milestones, and years of service and/or continue to be employed on the date an event occurs such as your company being acquired.

d) Benefits: Outside of monetary and health insurance, popular benefits for employees include work flexibility, additional paid time off for charity or projects, and paying for training or events.

4) Payroll/Health Insurance/401k/Help!

Just as you're getting ready to unleash the dogs of war and run your business, you realize that you have no idea how you're going to take care of your employee's payroll, retirement plan and insurance needs.

Sure you can take a quick lap or two around the Internet and figure out how to complete everything but you're ready to unleash the dogs of war, remember? What do you do?

You use a service that caters to businesses such as yours that will handle all of these services at once for you. Fortunately there are many such businesses and none are cost prohibitive.

Pricing for these firms is typically tied to the number of services provided for the number of employees you have. As you grow it pays to shop around to see if a new provider suits you better but that is a discussion further in your business's future.

5) Office Space/Remote Work

Does your business require a physical location? If so, will a shared co-location office suffice?

What are the ground rules surrounding remote work? Can all employees work remotely or just some? How do you avoid resentment if working rules vary based on job title?

Managing a varied set of employees with distinct needs is never easy. But adding in clearly defined rules of how work is expected to be accomplished offers additional complexity.

# CHAPTER 5 CHECKLIST

When building your product or service, it is necessary to think about the journey each of your customers, employees, partners, etc. takes through your business process.

1) Answer questions to determine what you need to create your end product. This is your input.

2) Clarify the use cases, or specific situations in which your business's product or service may be used. How do you, your users, and customers interact in those cases to allow your inputs to be transformed to your output? This is your throughput.

3) What does your end product look like and how do you interact with users after they finish using your product or service? This is your output.

4) Create a project schedule, checklist or notes of all activities which are required to complete milestones for your product or service creation.

5) Go through the list of all of the common items businesses require as part of their creation.

# CHAPTER 6
# SALES & MARKETING: WHO ARE YOU?

Sales and marketing are the fraternal twins of business. They may be born at the same time but they can have radically different personalities and needs. Yet, each of these twins needs the other, as different as they may be from one another. Companies can sell products without spending money on marketing, but no company can sell anything without defining who they are. Marketing at its core is the action of clearly defining who you are from every angle possible.

In Chapter 1: Be An Investigative News Reporter, we defined who our users are. When we think about marketing, we must also define who we are to all of the constituents or users related to our business. If you need inspiration to answer the following questions to help define who you are, may I suggest loudly playing the song, "Who Are You" by *The Who*[23] until the answers come?

1) Who are you to your customers?

2) Who are you to your partners?

3) Who are you to your suppliers?

4) Who are you to the community?

5) WHO ARE YOU?

Did you think a simple question could be so difficult? If you completed the prior work in each chapter, I hope you answered yes!

Once we define who we are to our constituents, we must complete our marketing plan. We created a business plan in Chapter 4. Complete Your Business Plan, which included details on our market analysis and sales and marketing strategy. We also answered some of the other questions a marketing plan requires in prior chapters. In this chapter, we complete the marketing plan to ensure that we have a solid story to tell for our business.

## MARKETING PLAN

The SBA provides a helpful marketing plan template, referenced here[24]. Following are the traditional sections the SBA lists on their website for the marketing plan, summary explanations for each section as well as my commentary. Note that some of the required work for completing the marketing plan was completed in prior chapters. If the section was completed, I will notate to use previously completed work.

## TARGET MARKET

The target market consists of the primary customer(s) you are selling your product or service to. You completed this information in Chapter 1. Be An Investigative News Reporter, within the "Who" section.

## COMPETITIVE ADVANTAGE

Describe your product or service differentiators as well as your value proposition. You completed this information in Chapter 4: Complete Your Business Plan in the Why Not Your Competition section. Rate your product and service differentiators compared to your competitors. Additionally, explain how important each of your listed product and service differentiators or value propositions are to your prospects.

## SALES PLAN

Details your strategy on how you will sell to your customers. Your strategy should answer the following questions:

## HOW DO YOU SELL TO YOUR CUSTOMERS?

1) Include a description for each sales method as well as the detailed journey each use case takes. To do this, detail the step-by-step journey information completed in the Throughput section of Chapter 5. How to build your product or service. Make sure that all parties that interface with the customer are included in this section.

2) Make sure to list out milestones for each sales method. For example, what is a milestone for phone-based sales and when is the milestone reached? Is a milestone based on the number of scheduled follow-up meetings or times that a prospect is reached in one-on-one conversation?

## SALES STRATEGIES

Following are sample sales strategy process summary explanations. Providing details is recommended, especially if you are trying to attract investors.

1) Phone: Call and set meetings with three targeted prospects per day to directly sell product or service.

2) Email: Each prospect will receive ten to 20 emails over a one to two month time period and emails will be sent using different email campaigns. Emails coincide with phone-based contact.

3) Online Sales: We are utilizing social media marketing campaigns and search engine-based advertising, online sales via demonstration requests, as well as direct sales.

4) Referral program: Sales expected from our generous referral program offering friends, family, customers and partners a percentage of revenue for each completed sale.

5) Survey/Quick Meeting: Surveys enable us to collect critical data from prospects based on different targeted users. Incentives will be provided to complete the survey as well as to set up follow-up meetings with a decision maker.

6) Customer Reviews and Testimonials: Word of mouth is critical for our business and each customer is asked to provide a testimonial for us.

   Note, not all businesses want or need testimonials but all businesses can use positive word-of mouth and referrals. If online testimonials are not a fit for your business, then try something different. At one firm that I worked for, the CEO challenged prospects in sales meetings to call any of their customers to show that theirs was a company to trust. Word of mouth can be extremely helpful depending on your business.

7) Repeat Business: We offer discounts for customers who utilize our service or buy another product within 90 days.

## MARKETING AND SALES GOALS

Specific goals are necessary here, for the next year and preferably for up to the next three or five years. To identify your goals, answer the following questions:

1) How much do you expect to spend on sales and marketing?

2) What do you expect as a return on investment (ROI) for sales and marketing?

3) How do you quantify the success of your marketing and sales goals?

4) How do you qualify the success of your marketing and sales goals?

Determining the amount to spend on marketing as opposed to sales is important. There is no one correct answer here but there are helpful guidelines. Here is information from the SBA[25] on how to get the most of your marketing budget.

As noted in the SBA article, how much you spend depends on your industry and specific needs. In my experience, spending 5-10% of your first year budget on sales and marketing is adequate but you may want to spend closer to 10-20% if you require lead generation to come from online advertising.

Another question that may come up regards your sales and marketing budget. Specifically, how much should you spend on marketing as opposed to sales? Of course this answer depends on your needs. In most cases, once a marketing brand is established it makes sense for the majority of the budget to support sales. Established brands may not require as much marketing budget, especially in situations where sales cycles are longer and complex. Once a brand is established, I recommend providing at least 60-70% of your marketing and sales budget to sales with the remainder going to marketing.

However, until a brand is established, I recommend the reverse with 60-70% of your marketing and sales budget going towards marketing-based brand awareness efforts.

## WHAT DOES BRAND AWARENESS INCLUDE?

When you are beginning your company, you will likely require branding, which includes the items listed below.

1) Search Engine Optimized Website.
2) Logo.
3) Color and font design.
4) Blog Posts.
5) Social media integration.

## SALES/MARKETING MATERIAL HIGHLIGHTING YOUR BUSINESS

1) An "About Us" sheet helps answer "who you are" as a business and why the customer should select you.

2) Differentiator sheet which shows your value propositions and your product or service's features and functionality as opposed to your competition.

3) Customized sales presentation to be used for presenting your product or service.

## PHONE AND EMAIL TEMPLATES

1) Rules of engagement determining how many phone calls, how many emails to send to prospects.

2) Key probing questions to ask as well as follow up questions.

3) Answers to handle challenges and common responses from prospects.

## MARKETING ACTION PLAN

Provide details on how you will achieve your desired results for sales and marketing. What is your price sheet and is it dynamic based on customer or service type? If you are using third-parties for assistance, explain how the relationship works along with a use case of an expected business journey through a sale on a step-by-step basis.

Explain how your pricing differs or is similar to your competitors. Detail all promotional programs along with response targets and goals. Are there any policies, regulations or laws that affect your action plan?

Explain how your target audience is expected to buy your product or service. Are sales successful because you spoke to the customer at the right time (impulsive) or because you completed a detailed Request for Proposal (RFP) for the customer (planned).

Explain the dynamics of pricing in the industry as well as with competitors. For example, if discounts are offered by competitors, do you have to offer discounts or can you include a different bundle than your competition to bypass the need for discounts?

Provide details if there are expected changes to the pricing structure in the future for you, your competitors, or the industry in general.

Finally, explain if you are selling based on your features and functionality, addressing weaknesses in your competition or industry, or fulfilling needs such as saving time and money.

## BUDGET

A list of all costs, including miscellaneous costs that are expected to come up without warning. Factor in at least 10% additional miscellaneous costs from your first year to be conservative. For the budget, include the following expenses:

1) Staff.

2) Third-party or contractor costs.

3) Media.

4) Search engine-based advertising.

5) Social media.

6) Public relations.

7) Revenue share or promotional pricing costs.

8) Product packaging.

9) High level bill of materials and fulfillment costs.

## MEASURE AND UPDATE THE PLAN

Track your plan on an ongoing basis. Review expenses vs. revenue at least monthly to determine if you are on track. If you deviate from your budget goals, is there anything you can do to course-correct?

Should you have partners or investors, it is advised to let them know earlier, rather than later, that the results differ from the budget and explain how you will rectify the situation. Perhaps your partners or investors have suggestions to help remediate any budgetary shortfall.

## DON'T FORGET ABOUT OPERATIONS

Although I kept the heading that the SBA listed for this section, I prefer to call this collaboration. As companies grow, different departments tend to focus on individual areas rather than collaborate. Ironically, collaboration is typically what helps smaller companies grow and it is one of the first things to disappear when true growth is established.

Have ongoing meetings with multiple departments to try and keep the special business you built as special as the first day you were in business.

# CHAPTER 6 CHECKLIST

1) Complete your marketing plan by finalizing the following sections:

   a) Target Market (use information from Chapter 1).

   b) Competitive Advantage: Rate your differentiators vs. your competitors.

   c) Sales Plan: Describe the different methods you utilize to sell to your customers with details on your milestones.

   d) Marketing and Sales Goals: List out your specific goals for a minimum of the next year and preferably over the next three to five years.

   e) Marketing Action Plan: Detail how you will reach your marketing and sales goals.

   f) Budget: Include all expenses you expect to incur within the next year at a minimum and preferably over the next three to five years.

2) Track budgeted revenue vs. expenses and adjust your plan accordingly (at least monthly).

3) Collaborate with your team to ensure all parties remain aligned on the overall plan.

# CHAPTER 7
# CUSTOMER ON-BOARDING

We are well on our way to reaching our goal of independence through our business's success. At this point in our book we have completed the following summarized key items:

1) Identified and created a boring, niche business that suits our needs.

2) Finalized and built our business.

3) Marketed and sold clients on our product or service.

For many businesses these are the final steps necessary to declare victory. After all, your business is successful now since you have customers and a means to attract more customers leading to increased revenue. What else is there to do? Quite a bit actually. You may have customers but are they so satisfied that they tout your product or service on social media and refer you to family and friends? If not, the customers you have today may not be around tomorrow and what if at that point in time, you aren't selling new customers as quickly as you used to?

The question then becomes, how can you make sure that your customers are so satisfied with your business that their referrals and repeat business ensures they will remain customers? The answer begins with a solid customer on-boarding experience.

## CUSTOMER ON-BOARDING: RELATIONSHIP BUILDING BY A DIFFERENT NAME

Every business and industry is different, but customer on-boarding is necessary for them all. Customer on-boarding consists of two unique experiences summarized below and followed by a more detailed explanation:

1) Customer on-boarding begins with optimizing the customer experience between the time the customer decides to purchase a product or service (pre-sale) and purchases the product or service (sale).

2) Customer on-boarding continues as customers interact with your business on an ongoing basis, building a strong relationship in the process. The stronger the relationship is between your business and your customers, the likelier it is that customers support your business through testimonials, referrals and repeat business.

## OPTIMIZED CUSTOMER EXPERIENCE

For all businesses, an optimized customer experience is key to making a good first impression. Just as we dress up in our nicest clothing for important life events, so must your business dress up for its most important event, impressing your customer.

In Chapter 5: How to Build Your Product or Service we discussed the importance of improving the journey users take through your business. For users who are first-time customers, that journey begins once they start interacting with your business as part of the on-boarding process. Let's use a service-based boutique gym as an example to determine how to analyze and improve an on-boarding process.

In our example, we have a small business boutique gym, with a unique niche in servicing men and women between the ages of 50-80 with chronic pain. The gym, Dennis's Gym, offers many options including flexibility training, stretching, mobility courses, small group and one-on-one training as well as weight-lifting. The gym prides itself on being a second home for members who want to improve how they feel, while reducing their chronic pain. The gym has an excellent online presence and an established method of attracting new customers.

However, the owner of the gym wonders if there are improvements to be made to his process. He asks his friend, Mike, to act as a secret shopper and take a journey through his gym from the eyes of a new customer.

## EXAMPLE: MIKE'S JOURNEY AS A NEW CUSTOMER

Mike follows the steps below to begin his journey through the gym:

1) Mike pretends that he is a typical customer of Dennis's Gym, a middle aged man with chronic low back pain. He goes online and searches for gyms in his zip code which helps with lower back pain. He finds several gyms but Dennis's Gym appears to be the only one that focuses on lower back pain for men. Mike clicks on the website link.

2) The website is easy to navigate and Mike instantly sees a large box in the middle of the page noting that the gym offers a free consultation. Mike enters his name, cell phone number, email, and information on how he hopes the gym can help him.

3) Mike's cell phone buzzes a few seconds later, and he receives a friendly message stating:

"Hi, I'm Dennis, the owner of Dennis's Gym

## CUSTOMER ON-BOARDING

and I'd like to schedule your free consultation to show you how we can help you. Take a look at the email we sent you describing our process and call, text, or email us with dates and times that work for your consultation. Have a good day."

4) Mike checks his email inbox. He clicks on the message from Dennis's Gym which explains the time-tested process that Dennis's Gym uses to help members like Mike. Mike grabs his cell phone and sends a reply text back to Dennis's Gym, letting Dennis know that he is available for the free consultation on Monday or Wednesday from 4:00 p.m. to 7:00 p.m. and from 9:00 a.m. to 11:00 a.m. on Saturday.

5) A few hours pass, and Mike receives a call from a number he doesn't recognize. He ignores it as it's likely spam. He receives a text message a minute later that states:

"Hi, I'm Mary from Dennis's Gym and I'd like to schedule your free consultation. I left you a voicemail. Please call me back or text me if any of the following days and times work for your free consultation: Tuesday, Thursday, and Friday between the hours of 8:00 a.m. and 10:00 a.m. We look forward to seeing you!"

6) Mike shakes his head as he looks at his calendar. The days and times that Mary gave him to schedule his

consultation are different from the ones he provided. He decides to send an email back noting that he can move some things around to schedule a free consultation for this coming Thursday at 8:00 a.m.

7) An hour passes and Mike receives a call from a strange number. He assumes it is from Dennis's Gym so he picks up. Jake from Dennis's gym calls to schedule the free consultation. Mike asks Jake if this Thursday works and Jake apologizes, as the earliest Thursday time would be in two weeks from now. Mike schedules the appointment for his free consultation on the first available Thursday slot.

8) A day prior to the free consultation Mike receives a text message reminding him about the appointment. Additionally, Mike receives a calendar invite via email to add the appointment to his calendar.

9) Mike goes into the gym and is instantly greeted by a front desk representative, who introduces herself as Mary. Mike explains that he is here for his free consultation. Mary provides Mike with customer intake forms, including liability waivers, for Mike to complete and sign. Mary tells Mike that Jake will be with him shortly for his free consultation.

10) Promptly at their scheduled time, Jake introduces himself and takes Mike to an office in the back of the gym to discuss how Dennis's Gym can help Mike.

11) Mike completes the consultation and exits the gym.

12) A couple of days later Mike meets Dennis at a restaurant to give his feedback on what it was like to be a new customer at the gym.

## PROSPECTIVE CUSTOMER JOURNEY

Mike begins by letting Dennis know that he was immediately impressed when he received a text message after entering his information to the gym web page to schedule a free consultation.

However, Mike also noted that there were many items which bothered him including the following:

1) Mike noted that it took a few hours to receive a voicemail from a strange phone number, followed by a text, neither of which were from Dennis. Mike felt like he was initially contacted by Dennis about a consultation only to be contacted later by Mary.

2) Mike also pointed out that Mary tried to schedule a consultation appointment with days and times that are very different from the times he provided. Mike wanted to know why Dennis asked for days and times when Mike was available for a consultation when Dennis ignored Mike's responses?

3) Mike further noted that he received a call later on from yet another employee from Dennis's Gym named Jake

to let Mike know that the time he would like to schedule for his free consultation is not available for another couple of weeks.

4) Mike let Dennis know that not knowing who his contact was made him feel like a number and not a customer. Mike told Dennis that if he were an actual customer he would have been annoyed and immediately ended the consultation.

5) Mike also asks Dennis why he had to fill out so much paperwork when he arrived for his consultation, only to have Jake ask all the same questions after he completed the paperwork.

Mike explains that in his experience, doctors' offices do the same thing that Dennis's Gym did by asking customers to complete information only to be asked the same questions multiple times. Mike flatly states that he knows that he has to go to a doctor to resolve medical issues but he doesn't have to go to a gym.

Dennis asks for Mike's help to make changes to the process and after some work, they come up with a brand new customer on-boarding process.

## CHANGES TO DENNIS'S GYM PROCESSES

1) Dennis starts by changing the outgoing text and email messages from his gym to better explain that he may be

busy working with other members to schedule a free consultation, but he will ensure that he or one of his trainers will connect to prospective customers as soon as possible.

2) Regarding the consultation, Dennis decides to no longer ask prospects to provide dates and times that work for them by text. Instead Dennis will only schedule free consultations by phone to begin the relationship building process directly. Emails will still be sent but not to schedule the free consultation. Mike helps Dennis modify the outgoing text message to read:

> "Hi, I'm Dennis, the owner of Dennis's Gym. We are excited that you reached out to us for your free consultation. I'm on the gym floor now with our trainers to help our members get long-term and lasting relief from chronic pain.
>
> We will call you shortly. Thank you! Dennis, Mary, Jake, and the rest of the team at Dennis's Gym."

3) Dennis also changes the customer intake process. Instead of asking for forms to be completed when prospective customers come in for their free consultation, Dennis decides to move to an online digital portal enabling customers to complete intake forms online or offline. Additionally, all prospective customers will be

asked by their trainer to complete the digital intake process prior to their meeting.

Dennis knows that not all prospective customers complete the digital intake process prior to their consultation, so he decides to have a tablet at the front desk that can be used to complete the process. He will still have paper forms ready at the front desk for prospects who do not want to complete the digital intake process.

4) Dennis also updates the process for prospective customers based on Mike's feedback, which he calls Prospective Customers' Gym Journey.

## PROSPECTIVE CUSTOMERS GYM JOURNEY

1) Free Consultation Request from Website

   a) Trainer on duty confirms receipt of the consultation request and is assigned to the prospect.

   b) Assigned trainer confirms that the outgoing text and email messages were sent from the gym to the prospect. If there are phone or email issues, follow the technical issues process in Dennis's Gym manual or contact Dennis for assistance.

   c) Assigned trainer calls the prospect and schedules free consultation ONLY by phone via direct conversation. Voicemails and digital messaging is fine but confirmation must occur directly by phone to build our relationship with our customers, the right way.

d) After scheduling consultation, the assigned trainer enters appointment confirmation in the system calendar and confirms that the reminder text and email message are set to be sent a day before the appointment.

2) Prospects contacting Gym via other means (phone calls, emails, unscheduled visits)

a) Trainer assigned to the front-desk answers the phone, email, or interacts directly with the prospect entering the gym. Introduce yourself and ask how you can help. The person calling, emailing, or visiting may be a prospect or it may be about something else. If a prospect is interested in learning more about the gym, provide one of our prepared file folder kits.

b) Provide a gym tour, making sure to show our aerobic, weights, stretching and group class's area. Finally show our cool down room and our one-on-one training area.

c) If you or another trainer has an opening, ask the prospect if they would like a consultation today. If so, have them complete the customer intake process (paper or digital).

3) Consultation Preparation

   a) Assigned trainer must review customer intake (digital or paper) prior to consultation. We need to understand our customers' needs so we can schedule an appropriate consultation and suggest a plan to alleviate their pain if they sign up.

   b) Based on the customer intake pain profile, create a customized consultation and workout plan using our detailed library of exercises. For special situations or any questions, ask Dennis.

   c) Place all necessary tools for consultation in the one-on-one training area. All equipment must lean on or be placed directly along the wall until they are being used in-session or group training.

4) One-on-One Consultation

   a) Greet the prospect and ask if they would like a quick tour before going to your office.

   b) In the office, discuss the information from the customer intake. Focus on how Dennis's Gym can help them with their goals and determine which of our membership packages makes the most sense for their needs.

   c) Complete consultation making sure to provide an abridged workout designed to help the prospects chronic pain areas.

d) After the customer leaves, wipe down and put away all equipment.

After going through this exercise with Mike, Dennis realizes that he must also update all of his other processes to ensure that he successfully continues to build a relationship with his customers. This leads to the second component to customer on-boarding, continual relationship building.

## SUCCESSFUL RELATIONSHIP BUILDING BETWEEN COMPANY AND CUSTOMER

As noted at the beginning of the chapter there are two different components to customer on-boarding. First, optimizing the prospective customer's experience between the pre-sale and sale. Second, continuing to successfully build a relationship between your company and the customer. You know that your relationship building is successful once customers are enthusiastic users. Enthusiastic users not only utilize your business but they also recommend your business to others via word-of-mouth, testimonials, or social media reviews.

Just as with any relationship between people, successfully building and maintaining a relationship with your customers is an ongoing process. In the example above, Dennis's Gym changed his processes for dealing with prospective customers to begin building a solid relationship with his customers. Dennis's Gym quickly realized that additional processes were required for all portions of the journey customers take in dealing with his business. Dennis's Gym also realized that it needed a better process of storing prospect and customer-based profiles.

It is one thing for customers to find and use your business but how you interact with customers based on their data, dictates how quickly you obtain your goal. Organizing customer data is simple in today's world through the use of Customer Relationship Management (CRM) tools.

CRM tools take a tedious process of storing and sharing customer-based data with your team. After each interaction with your customer, you can enter relevant information into a CRM to be accessed on demand by approved members of your company. Using Dennis's Gym as an example, all workout sessions can be entered along with progress and the mood of the customer. Storing customer information like this can lead to valuable insights for individuals as well as all customers through reporting. For example, Dennis may find out through customer interactions stored in his CRM that several customers have asked some of his employees about a weight loss contest, leading him to consider holding a contest for interested customers. The more relevant the customer information that is entered into the CRM, the more valuable the results.

CRM's are not required and a process that uses file folders to store customer information can be equally valuable. Regardless of whether you use a customer relationship management (CRM) tool or a notepad to track your sales intake information, make sure that you capture the following information:

## PROSPECT AND CUSTOMER PROFILE

1) Customer Information.

2) Primary Contact Information:

   a) Phone.

   b) Email.

   c) Contact Preference.

   d) Schedule Preference (e.g. contact on Monday, Wednesday only).

3) Other Contact Information:

   a) Information on all additional contacts.

   b) Include valuable customer insights (e.g. finance is the buyer but requires IT approval, yet IT is rarely available).

   c) Is there a sponsor supporting the purchase?

4) Relevant Information from Ongoing Interactions.

5) Billing information.

Once you have a profile for your prospects and customers you can ensure that your on-boarding process is complete. To accomplish this task, determine if you have organized processes to manage the most common customer interactions with your business. All businesses that hope to enhance their relationship with customers can benefit from this exercise.

Continuing with our example of Dennis's Gym, below are all of the organized processes that are required for his business to enhance his relationship with his customers. Note that each of the listed items requires a separate checklist schedule or step-by-step process to follow, similar to what was provided above in the Prospective Customers Gym Journey section.

**COMPLETE CUSTOMER JOURNEY FOR DENNIS'S GYM**

1) Prospective Customers

    a) Free Consultation Request from Website.

    b) Prospects contacting Gym via other means (phone calls, emails, unscheduled visits).

    c) Consultation Preparation.

    d) One-on-One Consultation.

2) Active Customers

    a) Lifetime Members.

    b) Quarterly Group Session Members.

    c) One-on-One Customers.

d) Maintenance Customers.

  e) Referred Customers.

  f) Graduated Customers.

3) Inactive Customers

  a) Inactive less than one year.

  b) Inactive greater than one year.

# CHAPTER 7 CHECKLIST

Optimize your customer on-boarding experience by focusing on:

1) The customer experience between the time the customer decides to purchase a product or service (pre-sale) and purchases the product or service (sale).

    To optimize your customer's on-boarding experience, start by gathering the work you completed on the customer's journey in Chapter 5. Then, go through this journey from a customer's perspective on a step-by-step basis. Are there any areas of improvement you can identify?

2) The customer experience from the sale of a product or service forward.

    Utilize a Customer Relationship Management (CRM) tool or alternative note taking system to gather pertinent customer-based information.

    Review to see if there are any common requests or patterns from customers which may help improve your business.

    Create processes to engage with prospective, active, and inactive customers.

## CHAPTER 8
# CUSTOMER RETENTION – A BIRD IN THE HAND...

Chapter 7: Customer On-Boarding, detailed how to analyze and design processes to optimize customer experience and relationship building, the keys to customer satisfaction. Customer satisfaction, in turn, is integral to retaining long-term customers who are instrumental to maintaining and growing your business.

However, customer on-boarding by its nature is a short-term process. After you sell to a customer, the customer engages with your product or service and the on-boarding process is complete. At the end of the customer on-boarding process you may have a completely satisfied customer; yet, if future economic troubles occur for that customer, it might lead to a canceled contract or decreased future sales.

Successful businesses know that they can always lose a customer, but having advance notice on the probability of losing customers is helpful for planning purposes. It is a process much like going on vacation and checking the weather before you go. You know the weather forecast may not be completely right, but you believe it is directionally right so you pack accordingly.

In this chapter we focus on customer retention, or the act of ensuring that we keep our customers. Customer retention requires gauging and aligning customer sentiment with business expectations. When a customer's sentiment is poor, it is good practice for a business to be aware and offer concessions or assistance.

After all, it is much cheaper to keep existing customers happy than acquiring new customers. According to this article[26], "Most research shows that it costs between six to seven times more to get a new customer vs. keeping the customers you already have." Plus existing customers can provide testimonials, referrals, and repeat business.

This is not to say that you shouldn't focus on new sales, as sales is the lifeblood of any business. However, it is common for businesses to ignore existing customers by focusing an inordinate amount of time and effort on procuring new customers. Perhaps this is human nature as we all have a tendency to take people and things for granted. A perfect example of this tendency to ignore existing customers comes from wireless phone companies. It is common for wireless phone companies to offer extravagant bonuses to new customers who sign up for service and little to few benefits to existing customers.

As a customer of a wireless phone company, how does it make you feel when this situation happens to you? If your answer is less than positive, think of this example whenever you think about taking your customers for granted. In fact, as it relates to your business, NEVER take your customers for granted. Even in cases where there are customers that you no longer wish to work on retaining, do not take their business for granted. At all times you and your team should be aware of your customer's sentiment to avoid surprises. Customer Sentiment can be determined through various ways such as the ones below.

# DETERMINE CUSTOMER SENTIMENT

## 1) INTERNAL CUSTOMER REVIEW

It is typically helpful for different members of your business to share relevant customer information on an on-going basis. Of course depending on your business, these discussions may only be required monthly, quarterly or even semi-annually, as opposed to daily or weekly. As with everything related to your business, you must make a decision of how and when to do an internal customer review.

Depending on your business, you may want to have different intervals for meetings based on a customer's sentiment. For example, your business may meet daily or weekly to discuss customers with poorly rated sentiments and monthly or quarterly for customers with highly rated sentiments.

Customer reviews should be live meetings, if possible, enabling customer information to be communicated directly among team members. Doing so allows for more information to be shared freely as opposed to relying on online meetings, conference calls, CRM systems or customer account folders. Topics of conversation for scheduled internal customer reviews include:

1) Current customer sentiment and confidence level that your team has regarding their sentiment.

2) Business metrics (metrics you use for your business such as units sold, transactions processed, etc.).

3) Customer goals vs. actual performance.

4) Resolving known issues.

5) Mitigating potential issues.

6) Process improvements or ways of resolving product deficiencies.

7) Customer-related items to be aware of (changes in the customer's business or industry that may affect your business).

8) Determining potential opportunities (additional sales).

9) Review important dates (contract renewal, customer-related dates to be aware of).

10) Prepare an executive summary with an action plan. Discuss merits of sending action plans to clients.

## 2) REQUEST CUSTOMER FEEDBACK

Customer feedback may be received through various means including customer discussions or surveys. Customer discussions and surveys are always a good idea, but how they are presented and the types of questions asked are important.

If you are unsure of how customers will react to surveys, tread carefully by asking select customers questions in a controlled environment. For example, call or email select customers with questions rather than hastily posting a survey on your website or a social media page.

Examples of survey questions to ask in a customer meeting or a provided survey are listed below. Note that you never want to ask a customer questions that you can answer on your own through research. Nobody likes someone who wastes their time. Remember, NEVER take customers for granted as they pay the bills for your business.

## DISCUSSION AND SURVEY QUESTIONS

1) How long has the customer used your product or service?

2) How often does your customer use your product or service?

3) How often does the customer expect to use your product or service over the next year?

4) How likely is the customer to remain a customer?

5) How likely is the customer to refer others to your product or service?

6) Would the customer be interested in being a reference or providing a testimonial?

7) How would the customer rate the overall quality of your product or service?

8) What is the customer's overall satisfaction level?

9) What are some products or services that the customer wishes you provided and/or would be interested in learning more about?

10) Is the customer aware of the product or service offering of your competitors? If so, what are some of the differences between you and your competitors?

11) If your long-term customer was brand new to your business, would they still choose your product or service?

Note that in cases where you have a business where customers purchase products or services on a one-time basis, surveys remain important but must be modified to suit your business's needs. If providing surveys to individual users is too awkward, ask fewer and more specific questions and, then, aggregate the responses.

## ONGOING MAINTENANCE

Maintaining a strong connection with your clients is the ideal way to ensure the relationship remains healthy. However, as important as maintaining good rapport with your customers is, it will not help you if you do not have an appropriate quantity and quality of staff interacting with them.

## WHO INTERACTS WITH THE CUSTOMER?

Do you recall the old expression not to put all of your eggs in one basket? It's good advice as one misstep can cause the basket to fall, breaking all of the eggs at once. Think about this expression as you look at who the primary contact is for each of your customers. If you have one primary contact for your clients, even if that contact is you, you are putting all of your eggs in one basket. This is a mistake.

You may know what is best for your business, but as will be described further in Chapter 9. Business Optimization: Future Resistant, you do NOT know the future. A month-long illness or a long vacation can cause massive ripple effects for your business if there is an overreliance on any one contact, even you.

To the best degree possible, cross train the staff or team members of your business on major tasks. Doing so will ensure that the business can easily maintain day-to-day operations should any one or two employees be out of the office or no longer employed with the company. The same rule applies for your customer-based contacts. Do you only have one primary contact for your customer? If so, do your best to get more contacts or risk breaking all of the eggs in your basket at once.

Additionally, it is helpful to vary the types of meetings you have with customer contacts. For example, your business's finance contact may have a one-on-one meeting with your customer's financial contact in addition to a team-based meeting with all contacts from your company and the customer. Of course you do not want to overburden your customer's employees or your own with senseless meetings, so make sure that the meetings are suited for the purpose at hand. The important point is that employees from your customer as well as your business are aware of multiple contacts to avoid an overreliance on one primary contact.

Listed below in this chapter is a subheading titled, How Do You Interact with Customers? It contains a list of meetings you can have with your customers. Use this list as a starting point to determine which staff should attend meetings both from your company as well as your customer's.

First though, let's discuss how balanced your team is.

## HOW BALANCED IS YOUR TEAM?

When customer retention is discussed, a couple of key questions typically get ignored:

1) How many of your employees are allocated to customer retention vs. sales?

2) What is the skill set of employees managing sales vs. customer retention?

Both customer retention and sales are undeniably important to a business's success. However, like an imbalanced see-saw, if the majority of your resources are managing sales or customer retention, the business will eventually have issues caused by the imbalance.

Similarly, employees well versed in customer success, account management, and customer retention may not have the desire or skill set to be in sales. Conversely, employees well versed in sales may not have the desire or skill set required to check-in with customers they sold to in the past.

As the business owner, resist the urge to jump to a conclusion that you need to focus more on sales or customer retention. First, determine if you have the right employees for the tasks you are assigning. If you do not, you must first rectify that issue by hiring, reallocating, or training employees to manage the tasks that require more attention.

Since sales are needed before any customers can be managed, sales will always be the immediate issue for your business, not customer management. However, once sales are completed, customer retention and sales become equally important, depending on the needs of your business.

## HOW DO YOU INTERACT WITH CUSTOMERS?

As mentioned earlier, you do not want to have senseless meetings as they only demoralize your customer's employees as well as your own. Yet, you know that you need to have some meetings to ensure that the relationship stays strong or if customer retention becomes a risk. What do you do?

The answer depends on your industry, business, and type of relationship that you have with your customer. There is no one best practice to handle all situations as it relates to interaction. However, there are ways of determining what will work best for your customer relationship. For example, during on-boarding you can let your customer know that your business finds having meetings on a weekly basis to be helpful for the first month of the customer relationship. After the first month, you find having monthly meetings works well until the anniversary of the relationship, after which quarterly meetings are preferred. Of course different purposes require different meetings, decisions that you and your team are best suited to make. Therefore, be flexible.

Following are types of meetings or interactions that will help you determine what works best for your company. Note that depending on your customer's needs and your availability, some meetings are best suited in person, while others make more sense as conference calls, video conferencing, or meeting over a meal or event:

1) Internal team meeting to discuss the overall customer sentiment. Preferably have this meeting with multiple employees from your team.

2) External team meeting with your customer to address any micro, or smaller, actionable items, improve results and discuss next steps. This meeting is best served with multiple employees from both your team and the customer's team.

3) Customer program review to act as a "State of the Union" meeting with the customer to discuss the overall status of the relationship and address any macro, or high-level relationship items. As with the external team meeting, it is recommended that this meeting consists of multiple employees from your team as well as the customer's team.

If you already have an external team meeting, to avoid overloading all parties with senseless meetings, it is recommended to complete a customer program review on an annual or as needed basis. Additionally, certain relationship-based materials, such as pertinent customer reporting, can be provided on a monthly basis even if meetings are held annually.

Depending on your business, a "best practices" summary may be a perfect addition to a program review. A best practices summary contains the best methods for completing tasks related to your business and industry. If you provide a service to customers, offering best practices enables your customers to not only determine how well they are performing compared to competitors but also can help them improve.

It is also recommended to showcase the benefits your business provides to customers in ways that make the most sense to their business. If you sell a vitamin-rich food product, and your customers are health conscious, let them know how healthy your product is by showcasing how your product is a substitute for large amounts of "normal" food. For example:

> To gain the equivalent benefits from our vitamin rich protein bar, you would have to eat 16 bags of potato chips, a loaf of bread, and a ½ pound of cheese. It may be better for your social life if you just have the bar.

You can even go further and point out that medical research suggests that ingesting the vitamins in your protein bar on average leads to a healthier lifestyle in old age, meaning less doctor visits and savings that could lead to $100,000 by the time your customer is 80 years old. Please check with legal staff before promising or promoting anything!

4) User manuals, Frequently Asked Questions (FAQ's) documents, instructions, kits, training, and procedural guides offer an excellent opportunity for businesses to ensure positive customer sentiment. Depending on your customer's needs, offering helpful tools for assistance purposes is always looked upon favorably. For example, let's say that in your business one of your customer's has a very specific request that is difficult to complete. By completing that task you are showing the customer that you will go to great lengths to build your relationship.

Remember, easy is not the point, building a successful business is. Many times you may have to go the extra mile even when it seems like it may not be helpful. My personal approach is to look at providing extra effort to customers the same way that I look at giving gifts. If I give a gift, I don't expect reciprocation.

If your business sells a product, like puzzles that come in a gift box, would your customers appreciate a handwritten note listing out things that go great with puzzles?

For example, hot chocolate, soft music, etc. Maybe, but maybe not. These are the extras you have to think about providing. Never worry if you have to abandon an idea if it is not received well. Just try another.

If your business has an online component, providing a troubleshooting guide may be beneficial as well, especially if your system reacts differently to different web browsers.

In businesses where your employees interact with customers on the phone or online, having prepared scripts detailing common scenarios is jointly beneficial for your business and your customers. For example, if customers commonly call to ask how to return a product, make sure that your representatives have a prepared script explaining the process. Having these prepared scripts for common scenarios, and practicing the interactions with your employees in a safe environment, helps maintain positive customer sentiment toward your business.

5) Automated reports may be well-received by customers for certain types of businesses. For example, let's say that you provide a service that analyzes data for companies to find unique opportunities, such as efficiencies or product combinations that have a high probability of being well received. In this situation, your clients may appreciate receiving a weekly automated report emailed as an attachment, which shows the top findings for the week.

6) Surveys offer another potentially beneficial interaction with customers. Let's say that your business has a great deal of experience in generating surveys and your customer needs help in generating surveys for their own business. Even if helping these customers with their surveys has nothing to do with your business, it is a good deed that will be well received.

7) Chapter 7: Customer On-Boarding, provided extensive information on the importance of customer on-boarding. Just as customers are on-boarded, so must they eventually be off-boarded. There are two parts to customer off-boarding and both offer important interaction points with your customers.

   a) Off-boarding is the process of a customer completing their journey through your business. Examples can include finishing a purchase and then exiting your site or shipping a product to a customer that is received. Consider off-boarding in this sense to be the last point a customer interacts with your business until the next transaction or product they buy, etc.

   b) Off-boarding is also the process of a customer leaving your business. Similar to how an employee leaving a company has an exit interview, a customer leaving your business can complete an off-boarding process. There is much to be learned for customers who no longer wish to use your business. Some helpful questions to include in an off-boarding process include:

    i) Why is the customer leaving?

    ii) What product or service is the customer going to use in lieu of yours?

    iii) How can you improve your product or service?

    iv) Would the customer consider using your product or service again?

8) Testimonials, reviews, and social media interaction can be helpful for both you and your customers. For example, your business can post enthusiastically about your customers on your webpage or social media. Likewise, your customers can offer testimonials, referrals, reviews or social media posts about your business.

These seemingly small interactions can add up over time, providing a jointly beneficial relationship between you and your customers.

9) Industry Group Roundtables or conferences offer a means to help customers network and improve their businesses or personal situations. For example, if you are a toy company, providing an opportunity to select customers to come to a conference to sit on a panel to discuss toys could be a once in a lifetime opportunity for both parties. Your customer will rave about the

situation on social media helping you with free publicity and marketing.

If your company is a business-to-business service company, setting up an industry-based roundtable for different business customers is looked upon favorably. These types of roundtables enable customer contacts to network and potentially find solutions that their companies can build together.

10) Partner meetings or consortiums is another opportunity to get your customers and partners in the same room at the same time. Again, different ideas make sense for different businesses. Depending on your business, hosting a conference or large meeting may be extremely beneficial to your constituents.

# CHAPTER 8 CHECKLIST

Customer retention is the act of ensuring that customers remain users of your business. Focusing on retaining customers is critical as it is much cheaper to keep current customers happy than it is to acquire new customers.

Customer retention requires the following items:

1) Understanding customer sentiment via internal customer reviews enables your team to discuss all items surrounding the customer, their business, industry and interaction with your business.

2) Requesting customer feedback via several methods including research, discussion and surveys.

3) Ongoing maintenance including value-added meetings between appropriate contacts from your business as well as your customer's.

4) Review your team to ensure that it is balanced correctly between employees who can assist with customer retention vs. sales as these are two different critical needs.

5) Review how your business interacts with customers and determine if there are additional services or offerings you can provide to enhance your probability of customer retention.

# CHAPTER 9
# BUSINESS OPTIMIZATION: FUTURE RESISTANT

Every successful business reaches a point where things are going extremely well. When your business reaches moments like this, it is common to reflect on how, after fighting for every square inch of your business success, you made it. When in this situation, many may take a long moment to celebrate and then get back to work.

After all, when you spend years nurturing your business, there are habits you absorb along the way that enable your success, such as not celebrating too long. Another habit contributing to your success is business paranoia, or wondering where or when your next competitor will show up, or if your business needs to implement changes to remain successful.

Your business paranoia may cause you to look around nervously asking yourself what else can you do for your business to maintain success. These thoughts are quite normal and there are some solid ways to prepare your business for future challenges. So, take a moment to relax and celebrate; then keep reading so we can make sure your business is future resistant.

## HOW TO BECOME FUTURE RESISTANT

As a business owner, you may consider yourself an expert in your industry and your market. But regardless of how much of an expert you are, you do not know the future. Nobody does. You may have set up a perfect business leading to untold riches and success, only to have it all come crashing down due to a deep recession or governmental regulation.

After all, how many lives were disrupted by COVID? How many businesses were irreparably harmed or destroyed? It was easy to be optimistic when COVID first hit our country as it seemed that it would only affect our lives for a short period of time. As I write this, three years post-COVID, it is clear that some of the changes COVID brought with it are permanent. There is no returning to pre-COVID times.

But putting COVID aside, things are always changing in the world causing a butterfly effect with domino-like impacts. Knowing that your business is not immune to the future and there is no such thing as being future-proof, what do you do? You optimize your business as much as possible so when the future hits, you are as prepared as possible and can focus on running your business in a normal fashion, rather than survival. It is at this point that your business becomes future resistant.

## BUSINESS OPTIMIZATION

From prior chapters you know how to on-board and retain your customers. Through the on-boarding and customer retention process you also know how to build strong relationships with customers, including identifying areas of how your business can improve. Finding and mitigating weaknesses in your business is a key step for business optimization. However important strengthening your business is, it is equally vital to keep your business optimized. Following are ways to accomplish this pivotal task:

### 1) MARKET RESEARCH

"The days are long but the years are short," is a popular quote about raising children. Many days feel like they will never end, but when your children are grown-up you look back and years have passed with you left wondering how the time passed so quickly. This quote applies to your business too. At times there will be work, like market research, you complete which seems tedious and unhelpful to reaching your long-term goal. It is true that you can research your market multiple times without gaining helpful insights. However, the few insights you do gain over time, more than make up for all of the wasted time.

One product I managed had a process which required users to physically sign (wet signature) and mail government forms to our company. Getting the wet signature from users was an onerous process causing a great deal of wasted time and money for all involved parties. The government was consistently against the use of electronic signatures for well over a decade.

Through continual market research we occasionally found minor changes to the process but nothing as impactful as the government allowing wet signatures. Then one day, while researching our market, a colleague found an obscure reference in pending legislation that, if passed, would allow the use of electronic signatures on the government forms we processed. As it happens, the bill did not pass, but now we knew that the government would eventually allow electronic signatures, it was just a matter of timing. Our company proactively programmed the system to allow electronic signatures. By the time electronic signatures were legally allowed, we were ahead of the competition by months, all due to continual market research.

As an added benefit, knowledge gained through market research may provide insights into product improvements or even different product ideas. Following are varied places to look for your market research. Also, keep in mind that as noted in Chapter 3: Within the Boring Niches, Lie the Real Riches, the library offers free access to many if not all of the publications listed below.

1) Trade journals: Industry-based trade journals or publications are well worth the cost to keep you up-to-date on navigating your business's landscape. Here[27] are some journals that may be helpful.

2) Alerts: Various online services enable you to request alerts for certain keywords or search terms. Alerts can be provided to you as often as you like. Here[28] is some more information on various alert sites that can be utilized.

3) Social media: There are some truly helpful insights to be gleaned from social media, among quite a bit of garbage. Finding good people and places to follow can be a life-changer for you and your business. Try various social media sites to identify which ones work best for you.

4) Newsletters: General business or economic newsletters can be worth their weight in gold if they provide clear and helpful information on your industry, customers and economic outlook. Here[29]

are some helpful business newsletters that you may find interesting.

5) Books: In his *Discourse on Method and Meditations on First Philosophy*, Rene Descartes said, "Reading good books is like engaging in conversation with the most cultivated minds of past centuries who had composed them, or rather, taking part in a well-conducted dialogue in which such minds reveal to us only the best of their thoughts."

The odd thing about reading is you never know which books are going to give you valuable insights to your business and life. In Chapter 3: Within the Boring Niches, Lie the Real Riches, I shared how impactful listening to Harry Chapin in concert was for me as a young child. Books work the same way, as you never know which book you read will provide you with an "aha" moment or unlock a different way of looking at the world. The only way to discover if this works for you is to choose a varied set of books to read.

6) Magazines: Physical magazines seem to be dying a slow death which is a shame since like books they offer valuable information in an easy-to-read format. Contained in this link[30] is a list of different business magazines, most with online and physical versions. As with books, reading a varied source of magazines outside

of your interests may be beneficial to your current and future business.

7) Varied news sources: Like magazines, newspapers offer benefits not easily found elsewhere. Having access to a variety of articles written by different reporters, offers a diversity of opinions and information. Finding local newspapers, in addition to national ones, is recommended, especially if you sell a product or service close to your headquarters. Here[31] is a list of newspapers to begin your search.

8) Trend analysis: Having access to trend analysis can be invaluable if you know what to search for. For example, if you sell wooden toys for children and identify that there is a trend for darker wood kitchen cabinets, you may bet that providing toys with darker woods can boost sales. Here[32] are some sites that offer trend analysis services.

## 2) DEMOGRAPHIC ANALYSIS

Demographics is data that shows information including age, gender, race, ethnic origin, and educational level for a population. This information is invaluable and must be studied carefully wherever possible. If a business is a boat, demographics are the oceans that determine how successful our trip will be. In fact, you can be a terrible business owner, in a challenging industry, and still have great success in business if the demographics favor your business.

Here is an example of just how powerful studying demographics can be to your business. Let's say that you sell T-shirts locally in California as well as online. The target market for your T-shirts are men between the ages of 25 and 34.

You consider your business successful as your profit exceeds your expenses quite a bit and you are able to live comfortably from the earnings your business provides. You read this book and decide to do some digging into demographics to see if you can improve your business. Below are the steps you can take:

1) You go to the census website[33] that contains all Census information our government collects every ten years.

2) Click on Tables and Maps (see below):

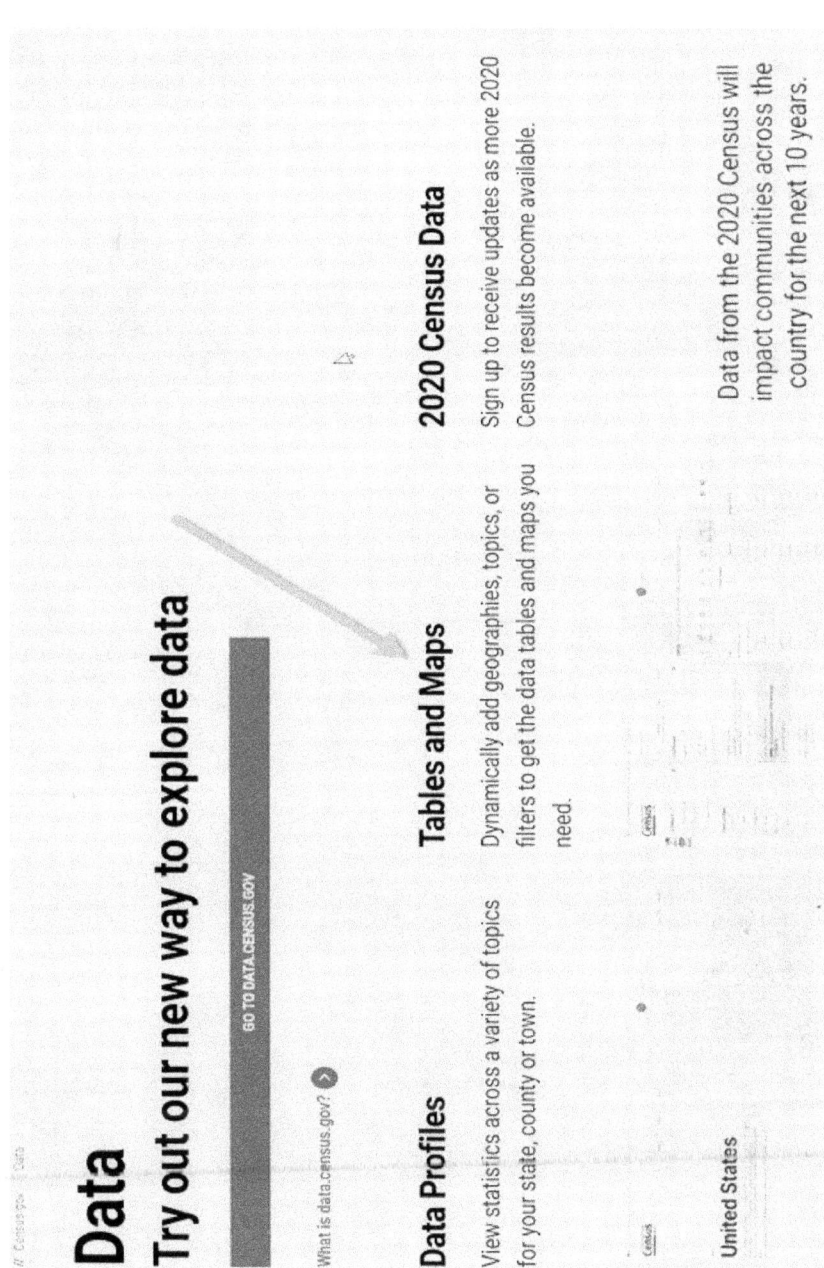

3) Click on Geos on the header of the table shown in the screenshot below:

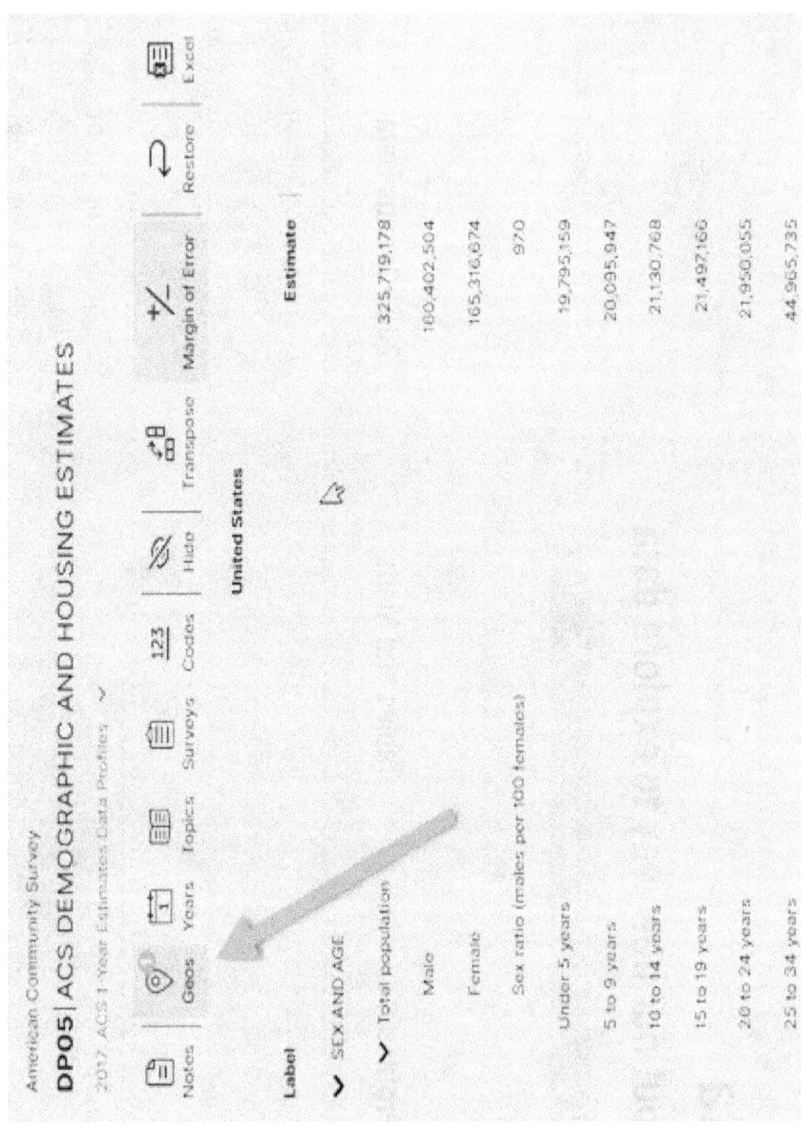

4) Click on State as shown below:

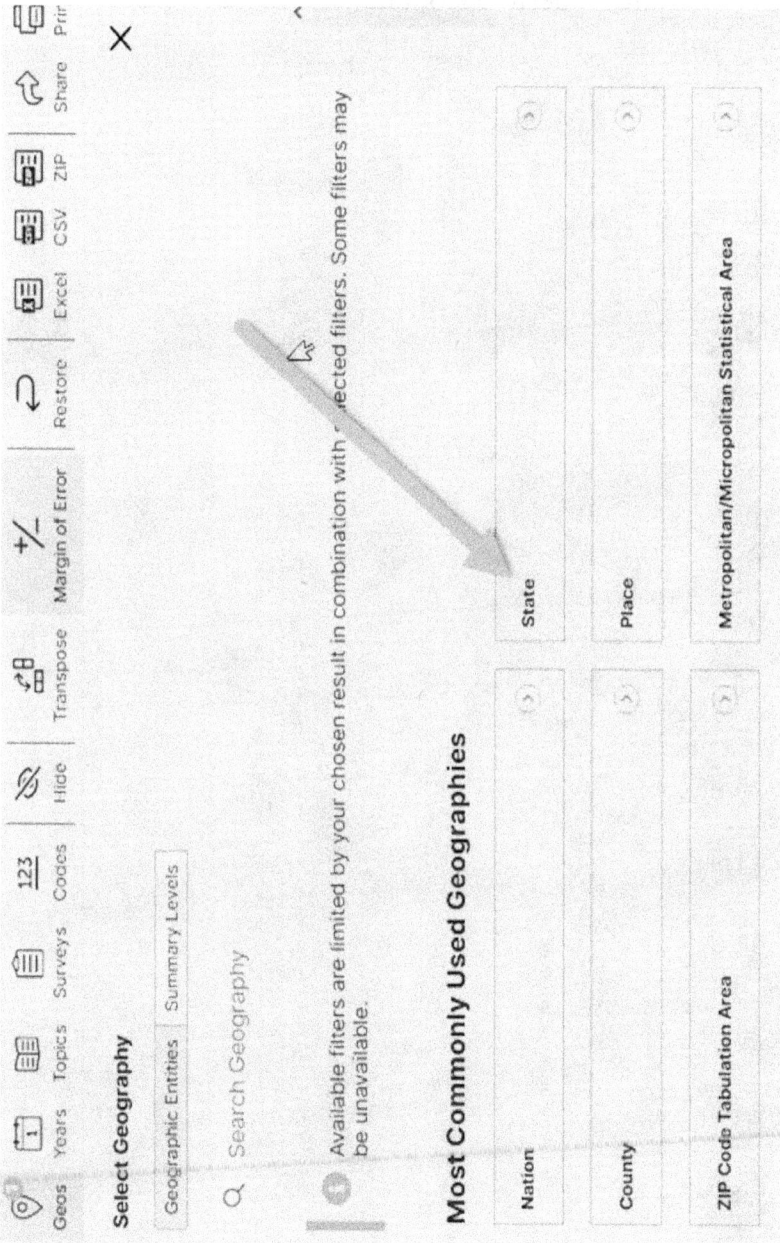

5) Select the checkbox titled "All States within United States, Puerto Rico, and the Island Areas"

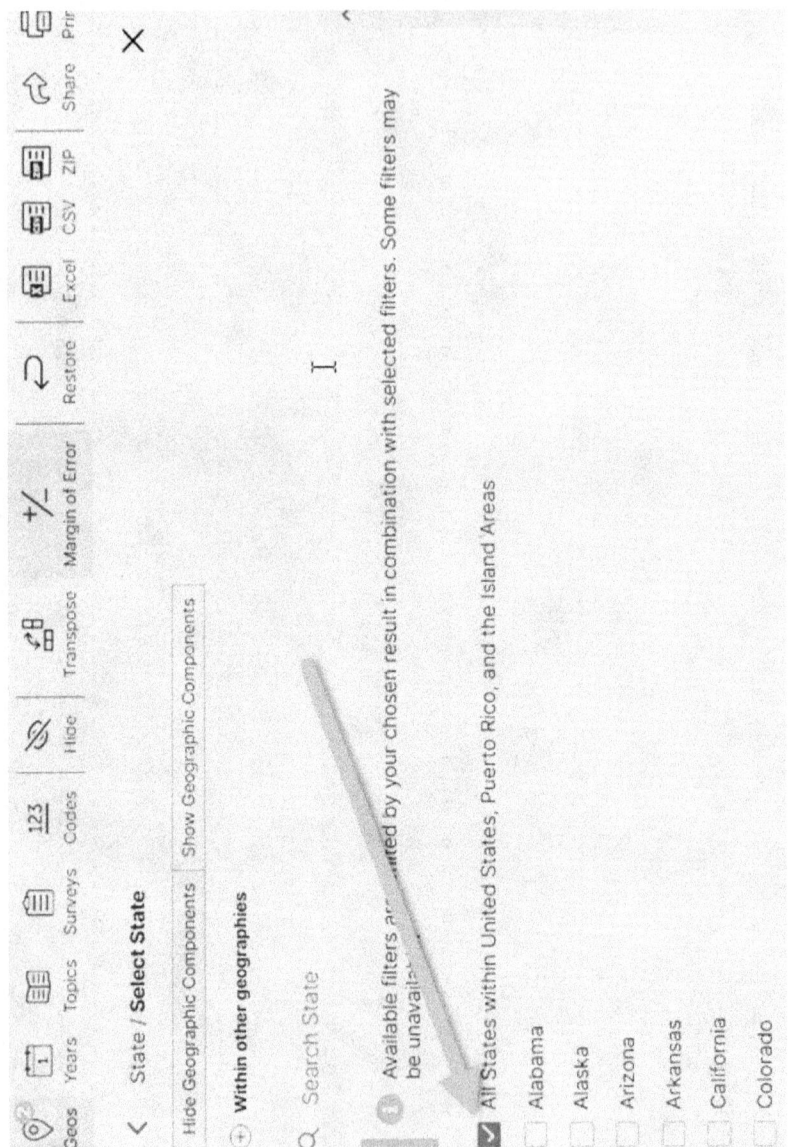

6) Click on Excel or any of the other download options to export and review all of the demographic information. See screenshot below for more information.

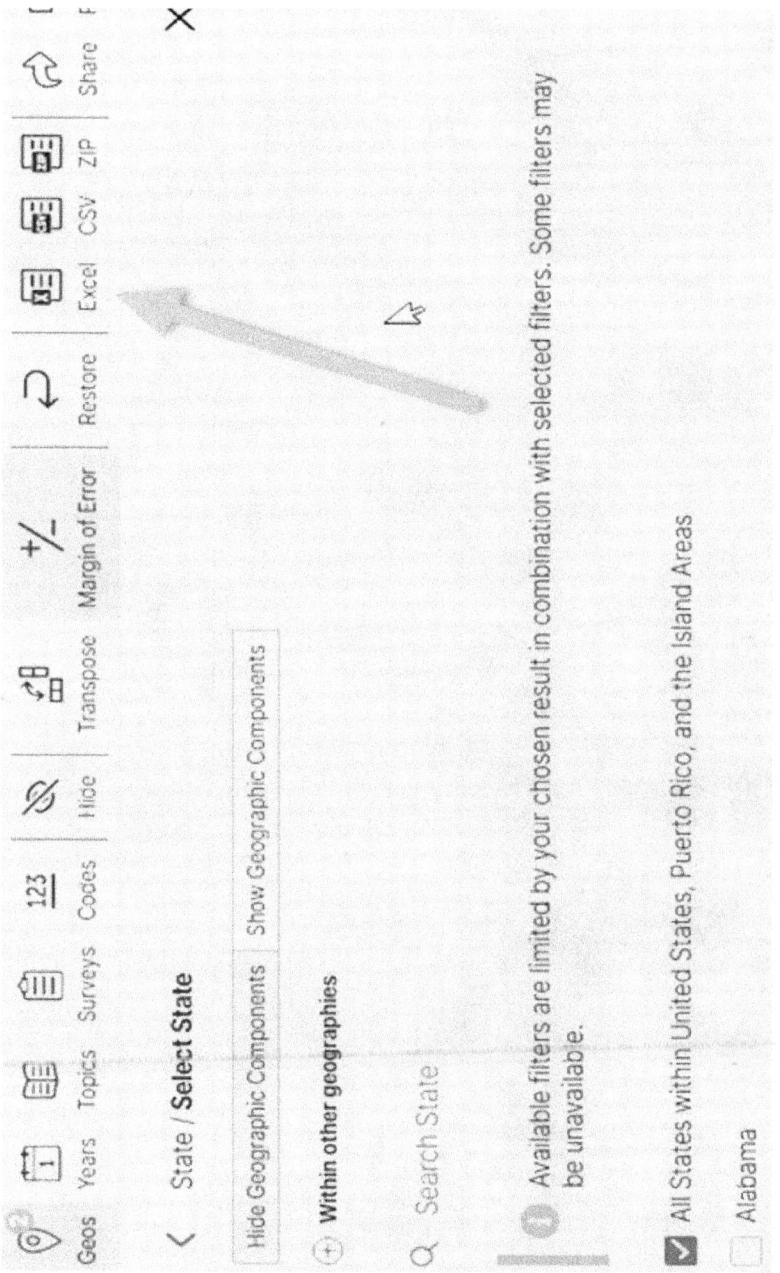

7) As shown in the screenshot below, open the exported spreadsheet and filter by the Label "25 to 34 years."

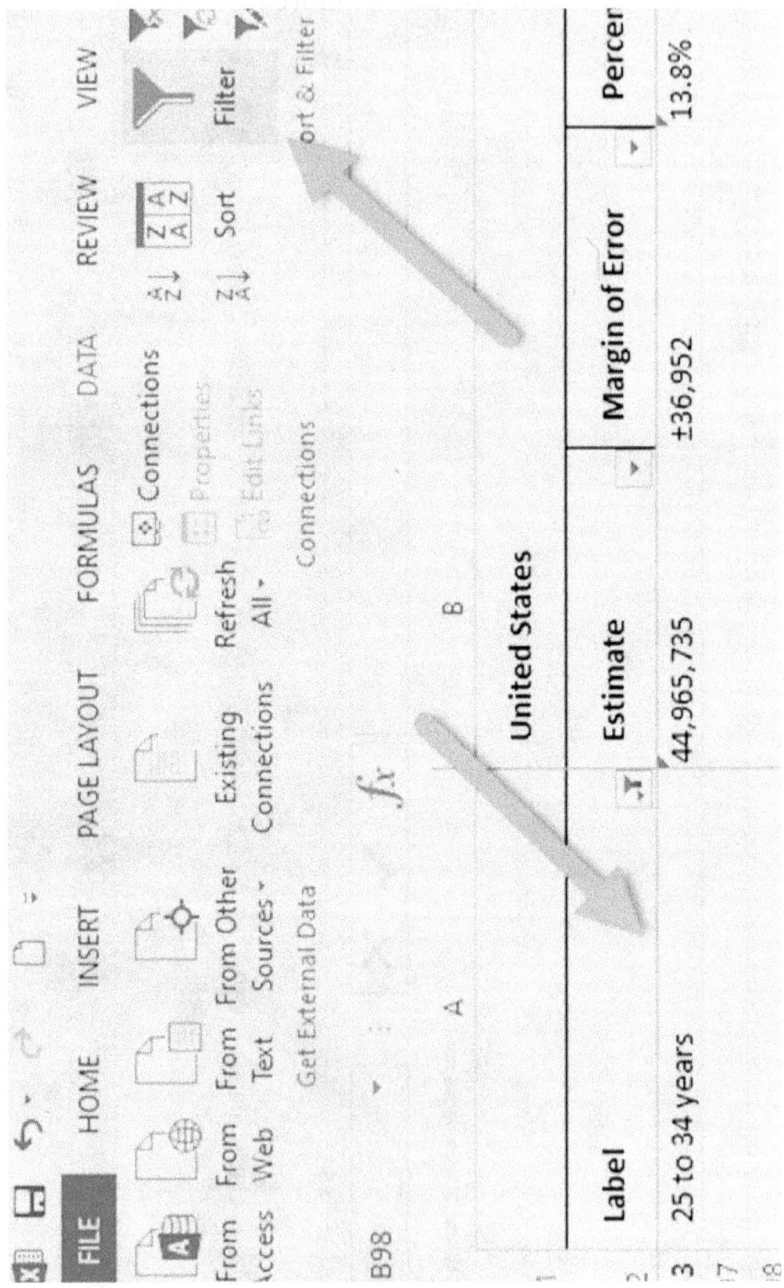

8) In our example, we care about identifying which states have the most men in our target market between the ages of 25 and 34. When we review the data contained in the filtered spreadsheet we find out that the states containing the most men between the ages of 25-34 are California, Texas, New York, Florida, Illinois, Ohio, Georgia, North Carolina, Michigan, Virginia, New Jersey and Washington. See table below containing the actual population data by state.

We are shocked to find out that all of these states have at least a million men in our target market as of the latest census information from 2017.

We quickly look at our sales data by state and find out that we sell the most products to California and Florida with minimal sales coming from the other states. Additionally, we find out that the number of our local California sales pale in comparison to the amount we sell to all of California and Florida.

We determine that it makes sense for us to spend more time advertising to the largest states, making sure to spend our advertising money intelligently by focusing on peak T-shirt season for states with colder weather.

| State | Male Population 25-34 |
|---|---|
| California | 6,018,225 |
| Texas | 4,122,739 |
| New York | 2,923,367 |
| Florida | 2,707,837 |
| Illinois | 1,765,429 |
| Ohio | 1,525,401 |
| Georgia | 1,421,366 |
| North Carolina | 1,352,154 |
| Michigan | 1,266,361 |
| Virginia | 1,165,166 |
| New Jersey | 1,162,394 |
| Washington | 1,105,343 |

The example above barely scratches the surface of what can be accomplished by using the demographic data contained within the census bureau website. Combining the census data with data from the BLS[34], and the local library, you now have valuable information at your fingertips to improve your business. The best part is all of this data is free.

## 3) IMAGINARY PIVOTS

In 1988, Andy Grove, the then Chief Executive Officer of Intel wrote a book titled *Only the Paranoid Survive*. As noted in this[35] post regarding Grove's book, I believe that Grove was saying that, "Constant evaluation, and transformation when essential is required for future company success."

In other words, imagine all the bad things that can go wrong with your business and prepare for them as best as you can. This is truly what it means to be future resistant. One helpful method to imagine bad things that can affect your business is to imagine how you could modify your business quickly. This is called pivoting, or the idea that you must change the products or service your business provides to improve or survive. One of the most famous examples of a business pivot is with LEGO[36] bricks. As this article[37] explains, the product had to navigate multiple challenges over its nearly 100 year old history. Then as recently as 20 years ago, the company was forced to pivot again. If you want to become a successful business, the work is never done.

Follow the steps in this chapter to minimize the chance that your business needs to pivot. Further, if the day does arrive where a pivot is required, you will be prepared with the completed work from this chapter.

Following are some helpful questions to ask yourself to prepare for necessary business pivots:

1) Assume you will go out of business unless you have a new unique product or service offering. What would that offering look like?

2) List out business ideas or changes obtained from the market research completed earlier in this chapter.

   a) Rank all ideas and changes according to which ones you believe to be most favorable to your business.

   b) Determine what it would take to complete the new ideas or changes.

   c) Ask or survey select customers to identify interest in the new ideas or changes.

   d) Add the ideas or changes to your roadmap if you receive a positive response from your customer base and the changes can be accomplished with existing work.

   e) Providing further information on the above point, it is recommended to stick to what works with your business, while working on new things. It is recommended to not spend more than 10-20% of your business time and capital on new ideas or changes, unless you are in dire straits. As important as changes and new products are, you must still ensure that your day-to-day business is able to run effectively.

3) List out the ideas or changes derived from the trend and demographic analysis noted earlier in this chapter.

4) List out the ideas or changes that can be derived from customer or employee input discussed in Chapter 8: Customer Retention: A Bird In the Hand...

5) Find truth tellers: as noted in Chapter 1: Be An Investigative News Reporter find truth tellers or devil's advocates to determine if there are things you should change to your business today. Finding helpful truth tellers, from among your constituents or network, is a critical part of any business's continued success.

6) What would you do if you were an outsider to your business? Ask yourself what changes you would make to your business if you could change anything without having to worry about politics or baggage of any kind.

## 4) REDUCE OR REMOVE DEBT

Optimized, or future-resistant, businesses must have a comfortable relationship with debt. This does not mean that you must use debt to build your business, but it does mean that you must be comfortable in how you use debt. Used wisely, debt can have massive advantages by helping scale your business in a much shorter period of time than if you were to grow organically. But the equally powerful disadvantage to debt is paying back the debt can lead to cash flow difficulties and business impacts, especially in times of stress.

In Chapter 2: Identify a Business that Suits You & Answers Your 1 H - How and Chapter 4: Complete Your Business Plan, debt was brought up as one of the many decisions to be made in building your business. The reason is simple, as you must first know how comfortable you are with having debt as well as having a strategic plan on utilizing it for your business. As with many areas of this book, there is no right answer for if and how to use debt, but there is a right answer for you and your personal well-being.

If you do utilize debt, it is recommended that you have an ongoing conversation with your lenders and investors on your business state as well as your vision for the future to combat potential future issues. If you do not use debt, it is recommended that at a minimum you have financing or a line of credit ready to be used for your business at all times, just in case there is an emergency.

Finally, it is recommended to always have at least three months of cash in your bank to run your business at all times. If it costs $25,000 per month to run your company, have $75,000 in your business bank account. Over time, build up a secondary cash cushion of another three to nine months' worth of short term cash, to be held in a bank-based business investment account that owns short term treasury bills or Certificates of Deposit not to exceed the insured limit.

## 5) OFFER UNIQUE INCENTIVES

When you look carefully at optimized businesses, they always have a secret weapon, their employees. Even for those that run a one person business, there is a secret weapon of a spouse, relative, friend or contractor who can be counted on to help the business.

Make sure that the parties you rely on for your business know how much they are appreciated. I am not talking about a $50 gift card and a pat on the back. I am also not talking about just money, although a healthy salary and personal bonus is always welcome. I am suggesting that to show your appreciation to your secret weapons, offer unique incentives such as the items contained below.

### *PROFIT-BASED BONUS POOL*

A profit-based bonus pool is separate from the individualized or personal bonus provided to your employees. It is a completely separate bonus pool which is distributed to employees based on the profitability of the business. The more profitable the business, the larger the share of the bonus for employees. Bonuses may be evenly split or based on title or years at the company. The bonus may be provided once a year or throughout the year, whichever makes more sense for your business.

One important note as it relates to paying bonuses is that, as the business owner, you must remember to pay yourself WITH your employees. Some business owners may have no problem with this idea as they always pay themselves first. However, there are many business owners who are so focused on taking care of their employees and others, that they pay themselves after everyone else.

This idea of paying yourself last is just as dangerous as ignoring your secret weapons. Why? Because just as with ignoring quality workers, ignoring yourself leads to resentment. Should you continue down a path of paying others first, eventually you stand the chance of growing such resentment that you dread coming to work.

Every complaint from an employee and every time an employee vents about something may send you into an unqualified rage where you ask yourself with thoughts such as, "By paying their salaries I can barely afford my lifestyle, and all they do is complain?"

Alleviate this issue by making sure that you pay yourself WITH your employees. Make sure that you are not skimping on your own salary and bonus. Also, if you have an extremely profitable year, share the wealth with yourself as well as your employees but not so generously that a slow upcoming year will break your business.

### COLLABORATION

Since Kindergarten we have heard that collaboration and teamwork is important. This is very true but your secret weapons are not stupid. Let's say that as the business owner, one of your employees offers an idea of a new product for your business and the idea leads to massive profits. How do you react? Do you tell yourself that offering the idea was part of that employee's job and do nothing beyond thanking them? Do you offer the employee a discretionary bonus? Do you offer the employee a percentage of profits from the idea?

These are difficult questions to answer, and as the business owner you must answer them. For those who may say the answer is simple and choose to provide nothing or a discretionary bonus, realize that the employee will remember the act and may not choose to share their next ground-breaking idea. There is a good answer of what to do and it typically is between not being greedy and not being taken advantage of. In other words, like we learn in Kindergarten, be fair.

# CHAPTER 9 CHECKLIST

Nobody can predict the future, making it all the more difficult to successfully manage a business through various economic, political and customer-based preference cycles. Optimizing your business is a key method to ensure that your business remains future-resistant, regardless of how the world changes.

To optimize your business focus on the following:

1) Market Research: Although tedious at times researching your business's market and industry will yield invaluable insights over time. Utilize the listed resources in the chapter to begin this process.

2) Demographic Analysis: Understanding the demographic-based data of your customers and prospects is critical to understanding how and when you need to modify your business. Follow the steps in this chapter to begin your demographic analysis starting with the free information from the Census Bureau.

3) Practice imaginary pivots for your business. To do this, imagine all of the bad things that can go wrong with your business and prepare your business for them as best as you can.

4) Reduce or remove debt: Debt is an extremely powerful tool to help a business scale quickly. However, in difficult environments debt can hurt a business much

## BUSINESS OPTIMIZATION: FUTURE RESISTANT

more than help. Keep aware of the level of debt and whether it is appropriate for your business needs and economic conditions.

5) Offer Unique Incentives: Keep your employees, partners, contractors motivated in your business's success with items such as profit-based bonuses, individualized bonuses and non-monetary incentives. Also, remember to pay yourself WITH your employees.

6) Collaboration: Determine how teamwork and collaboration will be managed for your business. Will good ideas be rewarded? If so, how?

# CHAPTER 10
# KEEP GROWING YOUR BIZ OR SELL?

Every journey ends. Inevitably your business reaches a point where events occur and the question arises, should I keep growing my business or sell it? This is also the point to mention that becoming successful and remaining successful sometimes require different mindsets and actions. After running your company for a long time, perhaps you need a break, or perhaps you have big growth plans but your partner doesn't agree. Maybe you receive a buyout offer that seems so great, you feel as though you must take it.

When faced with these situations, you must decide as the business owner, what the best course of action is. Below are some insights that may help, beginning with first asking yourself who you are without your business.

## WHO ARE YOU WITHOUT YOUR BUSINESS?

In the world we live in, many of us define ourselves by our careers. We don't start this way of course. As children we pursue various interests including sports, hobbies, and activities. We may have a diverse group of friends and enjoy each of them for their individuality. It is as though we are in a gigantic house with hundreds of rooms to enter, all of them open to us.

Then, as we grow older the rooms are blocked off or barricaded and we are left to explore only one or a few of the open rooms left in the house. To make it worse, we know that there are hundreds of other rooms to enter but we can't access them anymore.

Plus we may hear others laughing and enjoying themselves in the rooms which are now blocked off from us. We ask ourselves like the everyman in this article[38], "Why the hell am I even here?" Maybe we begin to hear the words from the prophetic song by *The Talking Heads*[39,40], *Once in a Lifetime*, "And you may ask yourself, Well, how did I get here?"

First off, I'm not going to say insipid advice like you are a beautiful butterfly who needs to spread his/her wings. No, this sucks! You just wanted your sports, hobbies, and activities and now you have responsibilities. But this is your life now and there is no going back.

Second, take a deep breath and before having an existential crisis go back to Chapter 1: Be An Investigative News Reporter and answer the 5 Ws and 1H again, but this time thinking from a life point of view and not a business person's perspective. The questions for this exercise become:

1) Who do you want to be?

2) What do you want to do?

3) When do you want to do it?

4) Why do you want to do it?

5) How do you want to accomplish your new personal goals?

Answering the above questions may crystalize some answers for you. Following are points to consider should you decide to continue managing and growing your business or if you decide to sell.

## CONTINUE TO GROW YOUR BUSINESS

Once you decide to keep growing your business, the existential crisis may go away, but the anxiety from running your business remains. This is likely a good thing for you as you are used to the anxiety as it's a feeling and a life you are comfortable with.

The best course of action once you make the decision to continue to grow your business is to make sure that your three to five year plan remains up-to-date in addition to the business optimization steps noted in Chapter 9: Business Optimization: Future Resistant. Also, be honest with yourself about when you expect to leave your business and what that will look like.

Answer the following questions:

1) Do you have big plans that require a large investment for your business?

2) Do you think it will take five or ten more years to grow to the level you want?

3) What do you do once you accomplish your goals? Perhaps it feels like you stopped your existential crisis from occurring but you really just delayed it.

4) Do you work until the day you die? If so, who takes over the business then? Even in cases where you started your business alone, if you have a family now, what will they do with your business when you pass?

5) Do you want to continue to grow the business because you're scared of what you'll do without it or because you cannot sell your business for the amount of money you believe it's worth?

It is also recommended to make sure that any partners, personal and business remain on board with your plans. It is common in relationships for a business owner to make promises to a spouse over time that boil down to, "Give me five or ten years and I'll sell the business."

Then, five or ten years pass and the business owner is faced with an existential crisis leading them with the continuous desire to keep growing. As the business owner, of course, you can make this decision alone, but you may be setting yourself up for marital strife by not including your spouse in the decision. It may not matter to your spouse if you have the best reasons in the world not to sell your business after the previously promised time frame, you broke a promise.

Even in cases where there isn't a promise to sell a business after a period of time, a spouse may believe that there was an implicit agreement that after a period of time, life would be different. This is not a book on marriage but having open conversations with all of your partners in life and business is strongly recommended prior to making decisions that impact others.

## SELL THE BUSINESS

In the 1978 Paramount film *Heaven Can Wait*[41,42], there is a dialogue about selling a business that struck me when I watched it as a child. In the movie, the former owner of a football team is lamenting to someone else about how the new owner took his team. Here is the dialogue from the movie shown in this clip[43] at 3:42.

Former Team Owner: "My team..." "That son of a bitch got my team."

Associate of Former Team Owner: "What kind of pressure did he use Milt?"

Former Team Owner: "Well, I asked for $67 million and he said okay."

Associate of Former Team Owner: "Ruthless bastard."

This summarizes perfectly what it can feel like to sell your company. You may get what you asked for but you no longer own your company. However, if you didn't sell, perhaps the business would have gone out-of-business within a few years. There are rarely clear answers of what the best course of action is but if you sell, know that what you built up over time is no longer yours and if the new owner so wishes, they can destroy your life's work in a moment.

Of course, there are great stories of businesses that are sold and the former owner is treated with respect and left to run the business. Anything can happen, but the odds of a happy ending may not be as good as you like.

You may end up as a "Queen for a Day[44]." What is that, you may ask? Well, it's from a television show that was popular when my mom was a child growing up in Queens, New York.

## QUEEN FOR A DAY

The television show *Queen for a Day*[45] picked a group of moms that competed to be "queen for a day." According to my mom, the competition consisted of each woman explaining how awful her life was. For example, "My five kids are slobs and my husband ran away," or "My mom can't walk and rings a bell for me to bring her something every five minutes."

My mom said that the winner became the "queen for a day" with a goofy looking crown and some prizes. My mom said she was horrified by the show but still she watched in utter bafflement. There also were mixed feelings when the mother of the neighborhood bully won "queen for a day" by sharing how awful her life was.

Why am I telling this ridiculous story about an awful sounding television show my mom watched as a child? It's simple. When you sell your company, in your head your name belongs in the same business books as Edison, Rockefeller and Jobs. However, the company that acquired your business might appreciate your skills but still treat you as the proverbial "Queen, or King for a day." However, instead of winning kitchen appliances or vacuum cleaners, you may win months to years' worth of scintillating conference calls and exhilarating conferences where you are trotted out like a showcase pony for all to see, yet ignored from any decisions of substance in the company.

It's enough to remind you of why you started your business in the first place. Again, everyone has different experiences and this may not be your experience if you sell your company. But knowing that this outcome is a possibility may help you act accordingly. If you are selling for money, know what you're worth, get paid, and be prepared to be treated like the queen or king for a day.

If you want to continue acting in your role and growing your business, but with support from a larger company with deeper pockets, make sure the contract stipulates your requirements. The contract should clearly state your future role along with remediation efforts if you are not able to run the business in the manner you were promised.

If you plan to leave the company that acquired you after you fulfill contractual obligations, take note of your situation. If you just sold your first business, you likely are a much different person at the end of your business's journey than at the beginning. Recognize this and answer the following questions after your 5 Ws and 1H.

1) Do you want to work for someone else?

2) If so, can you do so with limited or no autonomy or do you need to be the boss?

These two simple questions will help guide your next steps after selling your business. If answering these questions helps you to realize that you are truly a creator, then go create. If you determine that you need a break before starting a new venture, and you are financially able to take one, then take the break.

However, make sure that you have an honest conversation with yourself as to what you want to do next and start back at Chapter 1: Be An Investigative News Reporter.

# CHAPTER 10 CHECKLIST

Every journey ends, including the journey of your business. When the question arises surrounding whether to keep growing your business or sell it, there are several key points to consider:

1) If you plan on selling or leaving your business, think about who you are without your business. This is an often overlooked but critical component for any business owner. Answer the questions contained in this chapter for assistance.

2) Should you continue to grow your business, think about your future plans. This may require you to update your three to five year plan. Answer the questions contained in this chapter for assistance.

3) If you sell your business, recognize that it is no longer yours and you may not be treated in the manner you like. Should this be a concern of yours, you can contractually insert requirements about your future role.

Thank you for reading! If I can be of assistance, please contact me at forman@boringniche.com.

*"We did it Dad. I love you."*

—Scott Jason Forman

# ENDNOTES

1. https://www.bls.gov/bdm/us_age_naics_00_table5.txt

2. https://www.techtarget.com/whatis/definition/law-of-large-numbers

3. https://www.census.gov/data/datasets/2019/econ/susb/2019-susb.html

4. https://review.firstround.com/Theres-a-00006-Chance-of-Building-a-Billion-Dollar-Company-How-This-Man-Did-It

5. https://thedailyguardian.com/why-you-should-get-rich-slowly/

6. 20th Century Fox ; Lucasfilm Limited production ; written and directed by George Lucas ; produced by Gary Kurtz. Star Wars. Episode IV, A New Hope. Beverly Hills, Calif. :20th Century Fox Home Entertainment, 2013.

7. https://parade.com/1391976/samuelmurrian/george-lucas-net-worth/

8. https://www.techtarget.com/searchcustomerexperience/definition/TAM-SAM-SOM

9. https://marketingfoodonline.com/blogs/news/is-a-pie-business-profitable-selling-pies

10. https://www.foodindustry.com/articles/how-big-is-the-u-s-food-industry/

11. https://www.statista.com/statistics/237252/cereal-and-bakery-products-expenditures-of-united-states-households/

12. https://smallbusiness.chron.com/bakery-industry-analysis-64831.html

13. https://www.census.gov/naics/

14. https://www.barnesreports.com/manufacturing

15. https://info.nicic.gov/ces/global/population-demographics/how-many-people-have-ever-lived-earth-0

16. https://harrychapinmusic.com/

17. https://en.wikipedia.org/wiki/Verities_%26_Balderdash

18. https://www.sba.gov/business-guide/plan-your-business/write-your-business-plan

19. https://www.sba.gov/business-guide/plan-your-business/calculate-your-startup-costs

20. https://ascent.sba.gov/a0/1c/06d770bf46f382c83c2169fa424c/your-business-financial-strategy-3-1-financial-projections-tool.pdf

21. https://sa.www4.irs.gov/modiein/individual/index.jsp

22. https://www.sba.gov/business-guide/launch-your-business/get-federal-state-tax-id-numbers#section-header-5

23. https://www.youtube.com/watch?v=LYb_nqU_43w

24. https://www.sba.gov/business-guide/manage-your-business/marketing-sales

25. https://www.sba.gov/blog/how-get-most-your-marketing-budget

26. https://www.americanexpress.com/en-us/business/trends-and-insights/articles/retaining-customers-vs-acquiring-customers/

27. https://www.webwire.com/IndustryList.asp

28. https://awario.com/blog/best-google-alerts-alternatives/

29. https://explodingtopics.com/blog/business-newsletters

30. https://www.failory.com/blog/best-business-magazines

31. https://www.jumpstartmag.com/6-business-newspapers-you-should-read-to-keep-yourself-updated/

32. https://explodingtopics.com/blog/trend-spotting-websites

33. https://www.census.gov/data.html

34. https://www.bls.gov/

35. https://www.linkedin.com/pulse/what-needs-change-scott-forman/

36. The LEGO Group, "About Us," LEGO.com, accessed April 21, 2023, https://www.lego.com/en-us/aboutus/

37. https://www.history.com/news/the-disastrous-backstory-behind-the-invention-of-lego-bricks

38. https://hbr.org/2019/12/what-happens-when-your-career-becomes-your-whole-identity

39. The Talking Heads, "Talking Heads Biography," Rock and Roll Hall of Fame, accessed April 21, 2023, https://www.rockhall.com/inductees/talking-heads

40. https://talkingheadsofficial.com/

41. "Heaven Can Wait," directed by Warren Beatty and Buck Henry (Paramount Pictures, 1978), DVD.

42. https://www.paramountmovies.com/movies/heaven-can-wait

43. https://www.youtube.com/watch?v=-02AzkB2NPrI&list=PLjxSxa-j3hNfTFl74RNVcW7esvKhNlU9v&index=11

44. "Queen for a Day." NBC, December 30, 1955.

45. https://en.wikipedia.org/wiki/Queen_for_a_Day

www.ingramcontent.com/pod-product-compliance
Lightning Source LLC
Chambersburg PA
CBHW060317050426
42449CB00011B/2530